LUCA STEFANO CRISTINI

MAHLER
ICH BIN DER WELT ABHANDEN GEKOMMEN

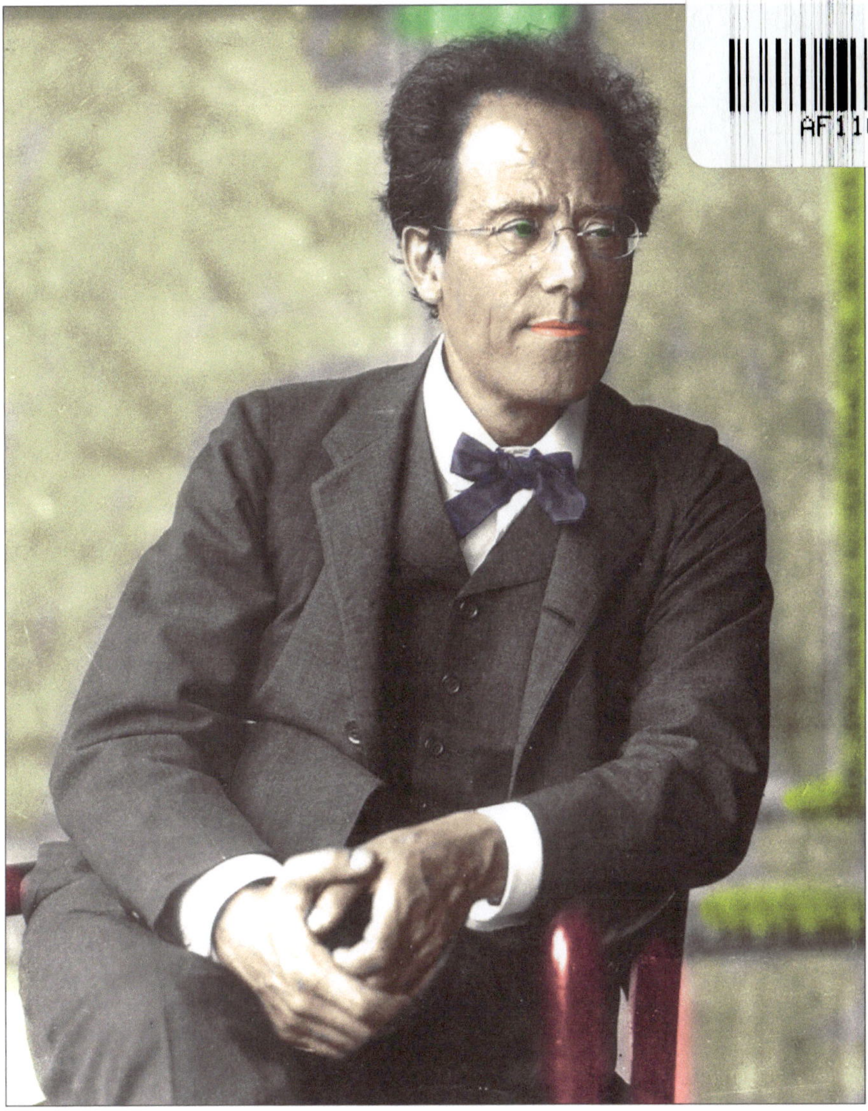

AUTHOR:

Luca Stefano Cristini, (Bergamo 1958) is an Italian historian, and historical illustrator with a particular interest in the XVII century history, (principally about 30 years war). He is also the editorial manager of Soldiershop publishing, an Italian publishing company specializing in military and illustrated history. He currently lives near Bergamo in North Italy.

PUBLISHING'S NOTE

None of images or text of our book may be reproduced in any format without the expressed written permission of Soldiershop.com. The publisher remains to disposition of the possible having right for all the doubtful sources images or not identifies. Our trademark: Soldiershop Publishing ©, The names of our series: Soldiers&Weapons, Battlefield, War in colour and Historical Biographies are herein © by Soldiershop.com.

To my Alma..

ISBN: 978-88-96519-95-0   1st edition: June 2016

Title **MAHLER - Ich bin der welt abhanden gekommen** (Historical Biographies 004)
By Luca Stefano Cristini.
Editor: SOLDIERSHOP PUBLISHING. Cover & Art Design: L. S. Cristini.

In cover: Gustav Mahler in Holland
At right Mahler at Prague with some friends.

In the last page an author portrait of Gustav Mahler

LUCA STEFANO CRISTINI

MAHLER
ICH BIN DER WELT ABHANDEN GEKOMMEN

PREFACE

ICH BIN DER WELT ABHANDEN GEKOMMEN

I chose the figure of Gustav Mahler as my study and Mahler's extraordinary epigraph is amongst the best written. The highlight of the entire collection is the wonderful *Ruckertlieder*. This quotation summarise and reflects the personal anxieties of Gustav Mahler:

I'm lost now for the world, where before I had wasted a lot of time; for a long time no one has heard of me, and maybe they even believe that I'm dead!
But if the world thinks I'm dead I don't give a damn. Because you really are dead to the world. And finally resting in a silent place, where I live alone in my heaven, in my love, in my song.

Gustav Mahler - Austrian composer and conductor born in Kaliste in Bohemia, in 1860, and died in Vienna in 1911. Sensitive interpreter of a world in crisis, Mahler brought the romantic language to a new phase of development, acting as a forerunner in the development of the dodecaphony by his protégés Berg and Schoenberg.
Mainstay of the music at the turn of the 19th and 20th centuries. An artist with a very complex problem and personality (he was one of the first to experiment with psychoanalysis by Freud).
As a conductor he reached remarkable fame, modern and extremely innovative for his interpretive style. His reputation as a composer developed fully only in the 60s of the last century. Mahler composed ten symphonies as well as numerous Lieder. He was the husband of the fiery and lively Alma Schindler, twenty years his junior. A troubled and intense union that strongly affect the life and creativity of this master.

This and much more is recounted in this book.

Luca Cristini

CONTENTS:

MAHLER

- His life   Pag. 7
- The man   Pag. 19

    Alma the bride of the wind - The other women of Mahler - Mahler on the Freud's couch

- The music   Pag. 57
- Complete catalogue of his works   Pag. 87

▲ Kaliste (Bohemia) the birthplace of Mahler, where the composer lived for only four months before with his family would shift to Jglau.
▶ Mahler boy of six years at Jglau, laying his right hand significantly on a musical score.

HIS LIFE

Kaliste, Jglau, Lubiana, Olomouc, Kassel, Prague, Lipsia, Hamburg, Budapest, Vienna and New York!

"I'm three times stateless: Bohemian for the Austrians, Austrian for the Germans and a Jew in the world. In short: always an intruder, never welcomed .. "Gustav Mahler

In an anonymous Bohemian village near the border of Moravia on 7 July 1860 Gustav Mahler from Bernhard and Marie Hermann were born. His family was of Jewish-Ashkenazi origin but they spoke German. His surname does not come from the German word *'Maler'* meaning painter, but from the Hebrew word meaning one who is circumcised. Four months after his birth, the family moved to Iglau. His father was a distiller, but also a carter and an innkeeper, however he had a certain fondness for music and it was he who influenced and directed his son towards a musical career.

His mother, an unfortunate woman, was assigned by her family to a tyrannical husband, although she was in love with another man. The result was a hellish marriage in which he found time to produce fourteen children. Gustav was his second son, following the death of their first, Isidor.

The childhood of Mahler was very sad, and he was devastated by the death of several brothers. Nine brothers were born after him and all died at a young age. Certainly these tragic memories had a great effect on his music through the use of different funeral marches and in desperate lied, especially in the harvest of the *Kindertotenlieder*.

Jglau

The first photo of Mahler dates back to the years at Jglau when the child was five or six years. It was a portrait of him next to a chair with a straw hat in his left hand while the right hand is significantly resting on a music score. Jglau during this era was a Czech town, but German was mostly spoken. As it was a military district, there were always marching bands, sounds of fanfares, trumpets and drums. These details the young mind of Mahler stored in his subconscious, carrying these memories to his music.

It was in the big house at Jglau that Mahler discovered a piano in the basement. He was so passionate that already at eight years old he had a small group of students. To his father, this was a clear signal. He sought the help of the pianist Julius Epstein, and thanks to him, in 1875 Gustav managed to enter the conservatory of the Institute of Vienna which he attended for three years. He obtained consents and aroused jealousy, probably due to his bad temper. In Vienna his most devoted friends were Hugo Wolf, Hans Rott, the brothers Rosé, and Rudolf and Heinrich Krzyzanowski. The friendship with Wolf, future great composer of lied was aborted due to the competitive spirit between them, the opera Rubezahl was written by Mahler but Wolf felt he used his ideas.

▲ Marie Hermann mother of Gustav Mahler, the unfortunate woman gave birth to 14 children, many of whom died in infancy. ▶ Bernhard Mahler who had the merit to understand the love for her son's music.

▶ The main square in Jiglau in a vintage photograph of the early twentieth century.

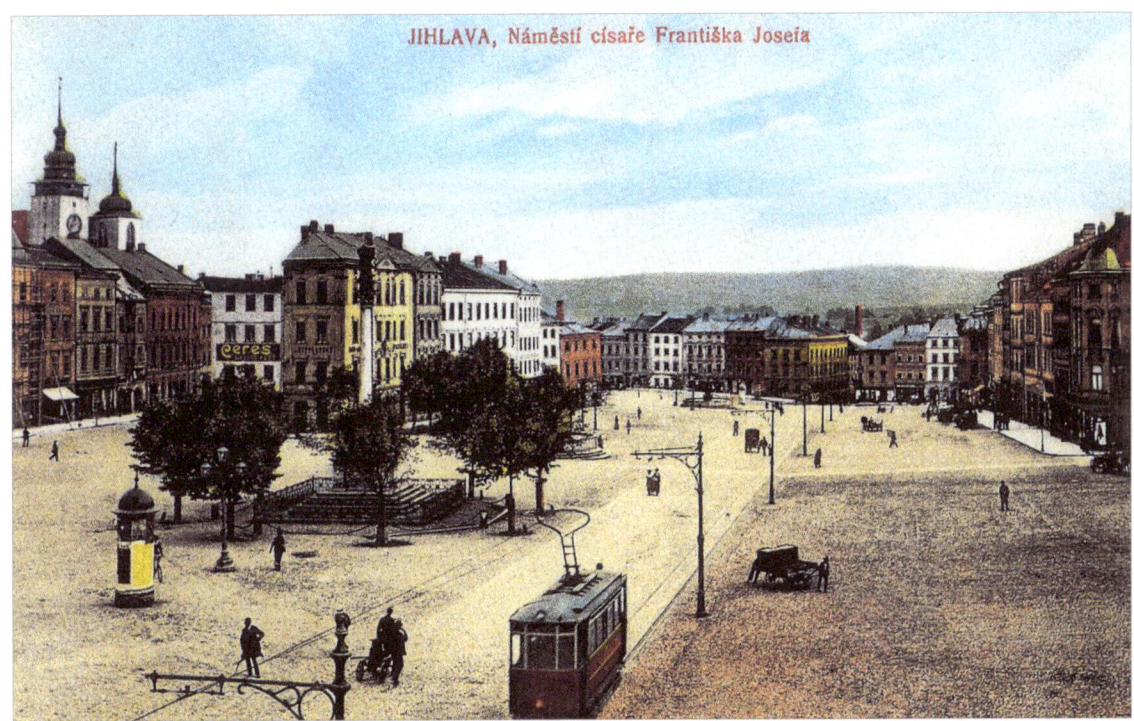

With Rott this strange creative symbiosis was even more explicit. The first symphony Titan in fact has many elements of a previous symphony written by Hans Rott. I refer you to the chapter that talks about this matter. The fortune of Gustav at the conservatory, however, was supported by the esteem of his professors such as Anton Bruckner, but especially Julius Epstein, his professor, who immediately sensed the great potential, so much so that he paid out of his own pocket the conservatory fee for the young musician.

The rapid career as a conductor

After completing his studies at the conservatory, Mahler had his first job as an assistant conductor at Bad Hall in the summer of 1880 where the repertoire was the operetta. Here the relaxed and light ambient atmosphere did not make notice of the young musician, who was already very serious and socialistic in spirit, and he took advantage of this position formally to compose his first works. In 1881, we find him involved in Ljubljana, capital of Slovenia and then at Olomouc in the early part of 1883, where we see a new bearded Mahler falling in love with his first love, Miss Poisl.

Still in 1883, but in August, Mahler was in Kassel, where he falls in love with the singer Johanna Richter who made him cut his long beard and grow a beautiful fashionable moustache. In an unstoppable crescendo and only twenty-five years old, Mahler conducted at the Prague theatre in 1885 where he directed Mozart's Don Giovanni. This performance found the warm approval of the old Brahms who at the end of the act saw him running down into the pit of the orchestra to hug him. Since 1886 he followed the Leipzig Opera where Mahler conducted

two seasons until 1888, following which he went to Budapest, the vice capital of the Habsburg Empire. During his years in Hungary, in 1889 Mahler lost both his parents and suddenly became head of the family.

His first act was to liquidate his father's company and distribute the inheritance amongst his sisters including Leopoldine who tragically died that same year. Now he was saddled with his brothers the reckless Alois, a compulsive liar who was always in debt. He eventually became a baker in Chicago and his brother Otto who too was a talented musician who committed suicide at twenty-one years, leaving a note saying: '*I give back my life to you.*'

He also had two sisters, Emma and Justine, the latter who Gustav had sincere affection, and who for a time took care of his brother.

Along with Justine in her role as the jealous sister/mother, Mahler stayed three years in the Hungarian capital. It is in the Hungarian capital that Mahler presented for the first time his first symphony. The following summer, after a brief visit to Iglau, he went to Monaco where he underwent surgery for the worsening of haemorrhoids he was suffering.

In Budapest, as would happen later in Vienna, jealousy and misunderstandings caused him to be removed from the Hungarian theatre.

At the station where Mahler was returning home, a crowd of admirers formed, many with tears in their eyes. A delegation of these approached the teacher and presented him with a silver wand that said: *To Gustav Mahler, the genius artist, from his admirers in Budapest!*

After Budapest, Mahler moved to Hamburg, the city of the Brahms, where he stayed from 1891-1897. Hamburg saw the disappearance of his moustache and the artist never grew this back. During the long years in Hamburg, Mahler met and became the lover of the Viennese singer Anna Von Mildenburg. This was always a stormy relationship which threatened to end in a wedding when the singer turned up with a priest at his studio and

▶ The Professor Julius Epstein with Bruckner among the first teachers to believe in the genius of Gustav Mahler.

▲ Above the house inhabited by Mahler when he was director in the Moravian town of Olomouc

▶▶ On the facing page the house inhabited by the musician in his years in Leipzig.

▲ Two photo portraits of Gustav Mahler, on the left with the revolutionary beard began to Olomouc and continued to Kassel, in the second on the right appears to be beardless that without a mustache in his new office in Hamburg.

surprised him. Mahler still managed to maintain the emotional outbursts of the singer who a few years later married a well-known intellectual of the Viennese Secession, Hermann Bahr.
Mahler converted to Catholicism, but this was forced upon him due to the anti-Semitic sentiment which threatened to block his career.
From 1893 to 1896, Mahler spent periods of his summer holidays in Steinbach am Attersee in Austria, the place where he revised his Symphony no. 1, composed his second symphony, sketched the third symphony, and wrote most of the songs of *Des Knaben Wunderhorn* cycle, based on a famous cycle of poems edited by Achim von Arnim and Clemens Brentano.
As mentioned later, in Maiernigg and Toblach, the musician composed his music in a small hut *Komponierhauschenî* by the shores of a lake. Over time, the little house will became the laundry of the nearby hotel and then eventually the Association of Mahler of Vienna converted the little hut into a small museum.

▲ Mahler's fourth from right in the second row, with looked vaguely Japanese .. Together with the orchestra of Budapest, when he directed the important Hungarian theater.

▶ The house of Mahler in *Aubenfrugrregasse* in Vienna.

▶ The *Wiener Staatsoper*, one of the most prestigious theaters in the world, represented the zenith of Gustav Mahler's career

VIENNA

In 1897, the thirty-seven year old Mahler received his most prestigious job, that of director of K.U. K. Hofoper (Imperial Royal Opera Court today known as Wiener Staatsoper). This was the most important musical structure of the Austrian Empire, and the world, and according to the Austro-Hungarian law this position could not be held by any person following the Hebrew faith.

Mahler, who never was a devout practicing Jew, converted for pragmatic reasons, to Catholicism. However, he did not become a practicing Catholic and only entered the church for his wedding and his funeral and he is often described as an agnostic. Despite this, references to the religious world are often present in his music, for example all of the first movement of the Eighth Symphony with the Catholic hymn *Veni creator Spiritus*. In any case, the spirit and his Jewish background remained widely present in all of his music, as is evident by the use of Klezmer themes in the third movement of the First Symphony.

The ten years as manager of the Vienna State Opera represented a real revolution for Mahler, and a big change in the way he undertook his work. Mahler was a real revolution in taste. Over these years however, there was a series of difficulties when dealing with the orchestra. They were not willing to tolerate the perfectionism and authoritarianism of Mahler, characteristics which were not well received by this team based on their traditions and status quo. Mahler had his own character, and countered against those who were steeped in the old ways of tradition, screaming *"Tradition is sloppy!"*

In Vienna, Mahler was not only the music director, he was also the first conductor of the orchestra, the artistic director and superintendent.

In the early twentieth century, Vienna was one of the biggest and most important cities in the world, the felix Vienna, the capital of a great multinational empire in central Europe and a very lively centre of arts and culture. Mahler knew many of the intellectuals and artists who at that time lived in Vienna, among others the painters Gustav Klimt and Egon Schiele.

His work on operas lasted for nine months of the year and for the three months of summer he would visit his villa in Carinthia in Maiernigg on lake Wrthersee and in this idyllic setting he composed four symphonies (from the fifth to the eighth), the *R¸ckert Lieder, Kindertotenlieder* (songs for the dead children), both based on poems by Friedrich R¸ckert, and Der Tamboursgísell, the last of his lieder *Des Knaben Wunderhorn*.

Immediately after buying his house on the lake, on 9 March 1902, Mahler crowned his dream of love courting Alma Schindler, the young twenty year old stepdaughter of the noted Viennese painter Carl Moll who was the second husband of her mother. Alma was a musician and an amateur composer but her husband forbade her

to continue to compose.

Alma and Gustav had two daughters, Maria Anna (called Putzi, 1902-1907), who died at the age of four of diphtheria during the course of the summer holidays at Maiernigg, and Anna (known as Gucki, 1904-1988), who, although falling ill of the same disease, was able to heal and became a famous sculptor and artist in her own right, and also managed to surpass the marriages of her mother Alma (who was married three times) by marrying five times.

Mahler met Alma at a dinner where the beautiful twenty-two year old was seated between two men who were both in love with her beauty. It was the painter Gustav Klimt and the writer Max Burckhard. The intriguing and reckless Alma, equipped with an irrepressible character and considerable intelligence had no difficulty in getting by in the company of learned men.

If anything, he could not stand that she was measured on her characteristics of beauty rather than on her artistic and intellectual abilities in which she was highly regarded. She also reasoned with

this thinking and ended up falling in love with Mahler who was not handsome or tall.

But he was refined and intelligent, and Alma fully grasped his genius. Alma was always in the company of men of high esteem.

The death of their child distanced the Mahler family from their lakeside villa, which was sold, and they bought a property as a summer residence nearby in Dobbiaco, Hochpustertal.

Starting from 1908 and for three years thereafter, Mahler composed his ninth symphony, *Das Lied von der Erde* and the unfinished Symphony no. 10.

Putzi's death was according to Alma the origin of her disagreements with Mahler, but it was in fact thanks to her vehemence as well as the age difference that soon serious problems of incompatibility between the two emerged.

There was also the tragic year of 1907, at the Vienna State Opera. Mahler was attacked by the anti-Semitic press that daily published corrosive satire on him. Among the most famous press, one called Mahler a scarecrow, a pun to reflect the continuing disagreements which he had with the majority of singers who were made to run away from the theatre.

Even the sympathy that bound Mahler to the modern dodecafonici Schoenberg and Berg, were viewed as dangerous and as a potential contamination, as Mahler did not appreciate that kind of music, although he did consider these characters as very talented. So even with the defence of the Emperor, at the end Mahler gave up and closed his collaboration with this prestigious institution.

Before accepting his new American engagement, he and Alma were granted a trip to Rome. This journey began badly because when they arrived in the Italian capital, their luggage was stolen. He even approached the queen who promised to resolve this incident. In December 1907, Mahler reached the United Stated of America following a long sea voyage.

Here he had his debut at the Metropolitan Opera House in New York on 18 January 1908 directing Tristan und Isolde. In America there also lived one of Mahler's brothers, however, Mahler refused to meet the wayward Alois Gustav.

Mahler's health started deteriorating. A heart defect was found almost by chance by the doctor who had attended the death of his daughter. Mahler grew old early, so much so that a quay customs officer when returning from the US addressed him as the father rather than the husband of Alma.

It was at their summer family retreat in 1910 that a serious marital crisis developed. Mahler, struck by the discovery of the betrayal of his wife with the young Prussian architect Walter Gropius, was advised to turn to Sigmund Freud, who met him once in the Netherlands and therefore could only give him some tips.

Freud, later, remembering the episode said, *I had the chance to admire the psychological penetration of a man who was a genius. He also suffered from obsessional neurosis.*

◄ One of the famous caricatures who saw Mahler as a favorite target of satire... Published mainly by the anti-Semitic press, it was at the origin, along with many other problems at the end of Mahler relationship with the important artistic institution in Vienna.

▼ Below the buildings of the Metropolitan Opera House in New York in 1905. This prestigious theater was the last stage of the great conductor until his death in 1911.

▲ Another series of the famous caricatures that the Viennese tabloid press devoted to Mahler.
► The death mask of Gustav Mahler was performed by Alma's stepfather Karl Moll the day after the death.

Following this huge disappointment, Mahler had a worsening of his general state of health. He was repeatedly forced to undergo delicate medical therapies, and turned in vain to famous specialists, however, they could not help but note the seriousness of his illness, a malignant and incurable endocarditis. When the situation became more serious, he was forced to interrupt his last New York season to return to Europe.

He then took a train journey from Paris on the Orient Express. Arriving in Vienna, Mahler was unable even to recognize his sister Justine, so desperate was his situation. He died in the sanatorium at Low of Vienna on 18 May 1911 and had not reached the age of fifty.

In his final delirium he repeated endlessly the name *Alma, Alma*, but his last significant words were *Mozart, Mozart!*

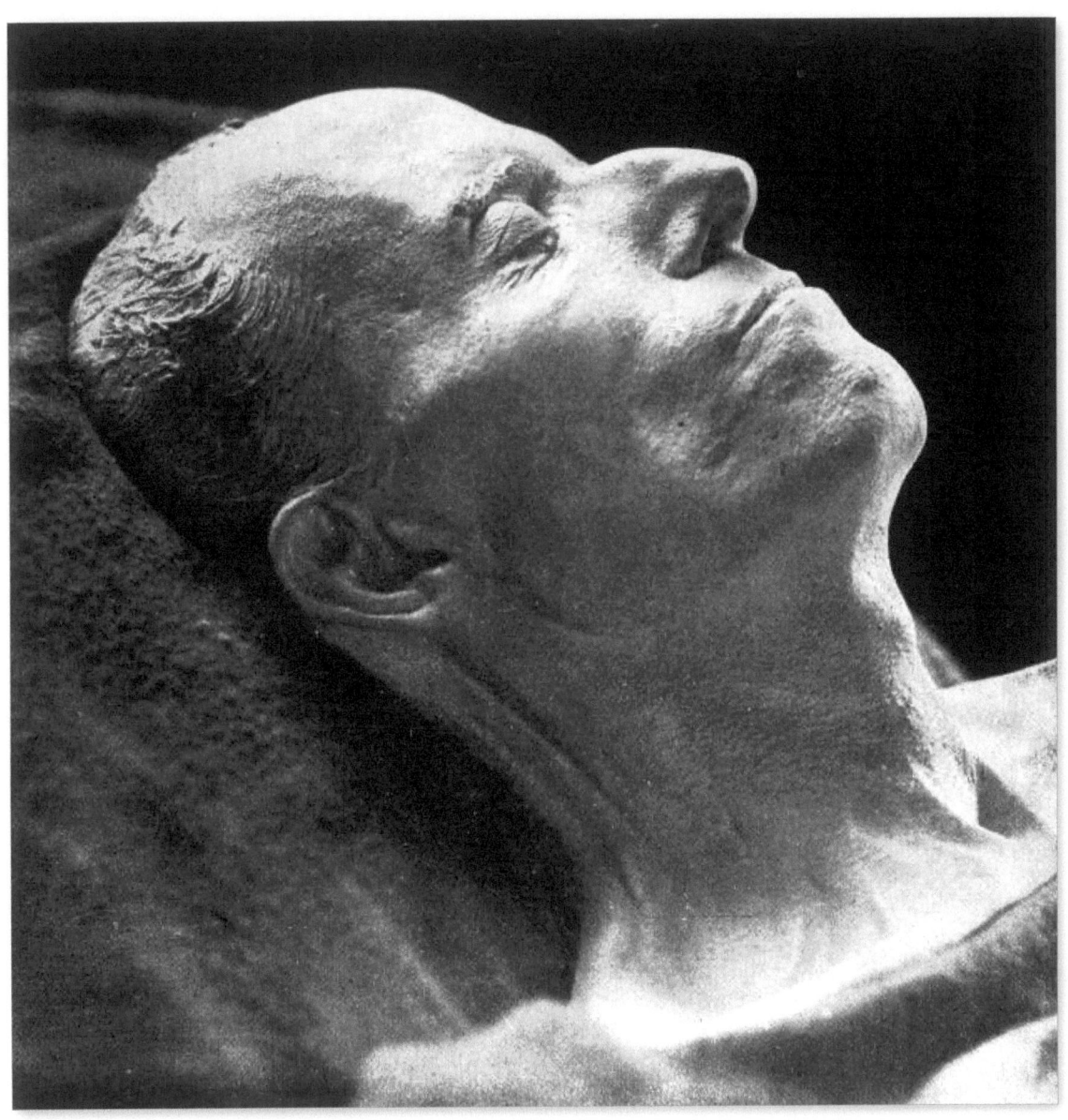

▲ Alma's blue eyes!
▶ Alma was the daughter of the famous Austrian painter Emil Jakob Schindler: Here we see her with parents in the garden of their home at Plankenberg in Austria in 1890, when the girl was 11 years old.

THE MAN

Alma the Bride of the Wind

"No one is ready without talent. Each must offer it in all its intensity, to seduce, to attract, to shine. It's a duty. Who needs help does not deserve to receive it?"

Alma Mahler

*A*lma, Almschi, Luxerl, LUXL, Almscherl, Almschili, Almschel until almost unpronounceable Almschiltzilitzilitzilied even my beloved child, my song, my Lux, my only one, my love my friend my Alma, my heart, love, breath of my life and so on, until the music: my Aeolian Harp! These are probably some of the many names and nicknames with which perpetually in love Gustav called his wife Alma.

It is important to understand that this woman had a profound impact on the life of great musician. Mahler spent roughly one fifth of his life with Alma, but they were the most definite and influential times of his life. Between the end of 1901 to May of 1911, Mahler composed symphonies from his fifth to the tenth as well as the famous lieder cycles of Ruckert, *Kindertotenlieder,* and *Liede Das von der Erde.*

Alma was a young scion of the Vienna's bourgeoisie. She was born in Vienna on 31 August 1879. Her father was the well-known landscape painter Emil Jakob Schindler. The painter became so famous that among his clients there was the Emperor. Thanks to his success, the family went to live in the sumptuous castle of Plankenberg in the middle of the Vienna Woods.

Alma always felt a special attachment to the father figure and since childhood he read her Goethe.

But he soon died in 1892 when Alma was only 12 years old. Her mother, Anne Sofie von Bergen, was a modest operetta singer born in Hamburg, who gave up her career to follow her husband. She was already three months pregnant with her first child (as will happen years later to her daughter Alma). Anna Sofie was a woman of a certain charm and seductive power who had a cheerful and lively character. A propensity to live an intense life.

In fact, the younger sister of Alma, Grete was not the daughter of Schindler. Alma discovered this only later in life, when her sister, with whom she was very close, began to give signs of instability when she tried to commit suicide three times. Interned, Grete then became suppressed by the Nazis, with the 3rd Reich's euthanasia program reserved for the mentally ill called Aktion T4. Grete was the daughter of an occasional lover of the mother, who probably had syphilis. After the death of Emil Schindler, in that same year, the Alma's mother remarried with another well-known painter Carl Moll who was a former student and disciple of her late husband. Carl Moll had already been a long time lover with undisguised nonchalance. The couple had two daughters. Moll was a blond giant to which

Alma did not hold too much sympathy, for obvious reasons. One does not marry the pawn when one has had the king.

Moll was in fact one of the most important founders and main organisers of the artistic movement of the Viennese Secession. Moll knew all the artistic cream and avant-garde of the city starting with his friend Klimt. His house became the nerve centre of the avant-garde artists of Vienna. Also thanks to that, Alma grew up in a very challenging and engaging artistic environment.

Alma was alert and intelligent, with unbridled beauty (at that time considered the most beautiful girl in Vienna), and for the early part of the twentieth century she lived a very rich and successful life.

The maverick Alma never attended school, she sang Wagner (whom she loved) all day, she did this with such passion that eventually she ruined her beautiful voice of mezzosoprano.

Her mother ensured her education. The educator, Max Burckhard, was a friend of her late father, and was a well known Viennese theatre director. He took this role seriously giving her lectures and even access to a whole library full of classics.

▲ Self-portrait of 1906 by Carl Moll in his study of the beautiful Viennese house where he grew his goddaughter Alma. Moll was one of the most influential artists of the Vienna Secession, and his house was an important cultural salon of Vienna.

▶▶ Alma young filly in all its irrepressible youthful beauty. This along with its remarkable seductive power have made her one of the most fascinating women of the time. Below Gustav Klimt in 1905.

He suggested Ibsen and Stendhal, but above all she favoured Nietzsche. So Burckhard, who is twenty years her senior educated and accompanied her to places and became a kind of second father to her, but with one small problem. This serious director lost his head for the young filly. Alma, the spoilt child liked to tease him, provoke him and then retire cruelly without ceding to him.

It would go better though with her second ace, Gustav Klimt, the prince of the Viennese painters. These great friend of her stepfather often frequented the house of Moll located in the elegant quarter of Hohe Warte. The big family house that was shared with another Secession giant, Koloman Moser Kolo. The great artistic movement will come to life in those years due to the dynamic Berta Zuckerkandl.

When Klimt met Alma, the girl was 17 years old, the painter exactly double her age at thirty-five and he was already a national icon due to his respectable reputation.

His first review of Alma: *A beautiful young Christian girl*.

Klimt at the time was a curious character, a maverick and unconventional. He loved wandering in his garden-studio wearing large overcoats, a kind of secular bishop's garment. Desecrated, original and brilliant he generated many scandals with his ways and inopportune choices in the bourgeois Viennese society of the time.

Alma frequented his studio and he '*devours her*'.... At least he tried to. She partly repeats the script already implemented with Burckhard, but this person intrigues her more.

The alarm bells started ringing and Alma was recalled to the fold by her parents. Seeing that this was not enough, in an attempt to remove her from this ogre, a close family friend took her to a trip to Italy. But it was not over. Klimt followed them to the land of Dante. He followed them from town to town pretending nothing had happened. The Molls believed his first explanation, believing this was a gross misunderstanding. Later, however, Anna Moll the mother discovered the diary of her daughter and in it the details of a certain kiss.

The measure is full. Alma's mother faced Klimt and ordered him to disappear as far as possible. But in Venice where they were, it was easy to play hide and seek. The streets of the lagoon city witnessed stolen kisses and longed for oaths. Once back in Austria,

Alma was dying to get back to her lover in the dreaded alcove of the artist's studio. Her precarious virginity was the last obstacle that slowed her down.

At this point, her stepfather Carl Moll intervened in a decisive manner and ordered Klimt to put an end to it once and for all. He threatened to also remove him from the Secession group. For Klimt this was a huge blow. Stunned and destroyed he could not do anything but give in, he wrote a letter justifying this, in which he recognised his fascination for and the magnetism of the young maiden. This interlude came to an end.

Several times after this they met again on several occasions, but Klimt responded appropriately and did not create further problems, but he maintained for the rest of his life for Alma that tender affection reserved for love that was not realised.

Alma was alone again with a heavy heart and sought refuge in music. Alma was placed with a professor who was small and ugly, Alexander von Zemlinsky. He was like Mahler a Jew and was also another genius. A great composer, he became increasingly noticed and had many points similar to Mahler, who will become one of his most ardent admirers. Alma started with Alexi her game which was well tested. She inflamed him and made him lose the light of reason. She kissed him, embraced him and teased him allowing him almost everything, but never conceded to him.

She considered him ugly, indeed a hideous monster, but was seduced by his depth, his culture and his eyes that radiated wit and genius. At the age of twenty-five years Zemlinsky already enjoyed the esteem of the Brahms and was a friend of Arnold Schoenberg, who later became his brother-in-law. Alma changed his life.

The two exchanged hundreds of letters full of daring promises and streaked with jealous phrases.

Certainly full of explicit passion. He at the height of excitement asked her for the infamous piece of paradise that he would never have. He wrote: *I have a lot to give, that others must always be forced to beg?*

Alma, and it is a feature that she will have for the rest of her life, was convinced that she gave more than what she received. For this she expected that her men would change, but not completely!

One of the last letters from Alma to Alexander summed all this up: *If you do not give to me totally, my nerves will suffer and the consequence will be terrible. Never forget when he touched me in my most intimate parts, a true torrent of fire! .... a small* (illegible phrase) *again and I reached the seventh heaven I wanted to kneel before him, embracing his naked lap and kissing everything, everything! Amen!* The precarious and fearless young Alma, however, was changing his life, and Zemlinsky would only suffer pains of love. Too bad for him that Freud was not yet operational at the time, and only started with Mahler the healing process of Alma's victims.

Outside the beautiful window of the villa on

▲ Alexander von Zemlinsky, brilliant composer and friend of Mahler and also one of his greatest admirers.

▶ Another alluring portrait of the fascinating Alma at the time the wife of Gustav Mahler.

the hill of Hohe Warte one could see the approaching figure in a black cloak the Director of Hofoper of Vienna Gustav Mahler.

The man that was sneaking into Alma's life, just to reiterate was a genius, even more so than the others. Gustav Mahler, for four years now director of the Opera of Corte is one that through his stature, reputation and ambition was well known in Vienna. A good picking for our young but tough Alma, indeed a challenge. The whole city was talking about his musical talents either complementing him, critizing him or considering him a villain. But he was always on everybody's lips, it was a topic either for the living room or the tavern. The court and the emperor worshiped him and this was his best insurance coverage. Francis Joseph states: *Mahler I have appointed, and woe to anyone who touches him!* This esteem and fame he enjoyed are mainly attributed to his being director, and much less to his role as a composer.

Small, neurotic, never still, with his nails perpetually bitten and always agitated. The character lends itself to the eye. Alma has left us with an effective aphorism about Mahler's restlessness: *When you were with him it was like there was always a corpse under the table! Furthermore he had a strange way of moving, his walk was lopsided, asymmetrical and irregular. He stomped his foot like horses do. He always pointed his face forward like a sniffer dog when they are hunting their prey.* An unidentified face, at times elegant and stately at other times sulphurous, demonic but always interesting. He had a strong voice in contrast to his contrite stature. Hairless, without a moustache and beard in the years when these were very popular. He was also always distracted and forgot things. Sometimes he forgot important things, but almost always he forgot his hat anywhere on benches or at the station, headgear which mischievous children enjoyed to give back to him, chasing this kind of clown with jokes and shouting, as he passed through the parks and gardens of the imperial capital.

Often unkempt and dishevelled, his hair was never combed and went everywhere. He did not have the gift of elegance, even when he could afford expensive clothes, he worn these with little grace. He liked to take long walks and walked to work. On one of these walks he met workers marching to protest some injustice and without delay he joined them. Unlike Alma, Mahler had a socialist heart.

To hold his prestigious assignment at the Opera, Mahler also converted to Catholicism. An act that he had to do in order to get and maintain his job. Yet his intimate religious inspiration were always much closer to Christianity rather than Judaism. Also in this case Alma wrote with sarcasm: *Gustav communicates with God by telephone.*

His wife also said that Mahler had no sense of humour and was gullible.

In truth, the master has left numerous extracts of letters to friends, girlfriends, and colleagues in which one can appreciate this art of self irony. For example, with regards to his haemorrhoids that will torture him all his life, and that forced him to stop continuously at toilets she loved to joke: *Gustav Mahler has finally had the fate he deserves, staying in toilets as a result of the countless combined troubles.*

Finally, although he had many invitations, Mahler did not like high society and was not interested in meeting new people, he already had his hands full with musicians and singers!

The exception was Berta Zuckerkandl, who through her famous salon Mahler met his future lover.

▲ The Mahler couple n the last years of their relationship walking serenely in Dobbiaco meadows, where soon will break the drama due to the betrayal of Alma for the future great Bauhaus architect Walter Gropius.
◀ Photo portrait of Gustav Mahler in the years when he met his future wife, Alma.

Word of honour?

November 1901, after a failed attempt, Berta succeeded to organise an evening in her salon with amongst others, Alma and Gustav. It was the first time that the two met.
In this meeting, there were other acquaintances of Alma, namely Gustav Klimt her old lover and Max Burckhard her old educator. The latter did not have any sympathy for Mahler. Alma was radiant and beautiful, and she manoeuvred between her two old flames. Alma had a slight defect, she had little hearing in one of her ears and as a result she would extend her face towards the speaker in such a seductive way that gave the impression to the person that he was the centre of her world!
Mahler was sitting in the front and the mood and chat was lively and carefree. Alma recalled that the director of the Opera peered at her throughout the evening from behind his round glasses. At the end of the dinner, he found a way to get closer to her and broke the ice. In a crescendo of theatre the two started squabbling. Alma accused of not having yet read the score made to her by Zemlinsky for quite some time: *You do not decide to represent the ballet, the golden heart of Zemlinsky. But I had promised!* And Mahler replied: *and such a cheap ballet, incomprehensible.* Alma objected: *this is a masterpiece, Zemlinsky himself explained to me the symbolism of his book. Would you like me to explain? I am all ears* Mahler replied with loving irony meanwhile he devoured her with his eyes.
Alma foiled the blow and secured the winning blow: *But can you please explain the meaning of the Korean girlfriend.*
It was a horrible ballet and incomprehensible that it became a permanent billboard in Vienna. With bursts of laughter between the two they then lowered their tone which unknowingly to the two began their amorous adventure.

At the end he asked where she lived. In Hohe Warte at the foot of the hill replied Alma. Mahler volunteered to accompany her, but Alma declined his offer. Mahler was assured then a visit to the Opera, she agreed and he concluded with the expression: *word of honour?* followed by a clear nod from Alma. The following days Mahler wrote his first letters to her. The following extracts demonstrate how the relationship developed between these two lovers.

On 28 November 1901 (the day after their meeting): *I have collected in a hurry for you my dear lady Alma, my compositions etc.*

On 4 December: *My dearest friend signed yours Gustav Mahler.*

8 December *Dearest Almschileri you gave me a true joy!* And finally the 12 December: *My Dear beloved bambinatutto that lives in me, I am dedicated to you signed yours truly Gustavî.* There is that saying to burn bridges in less than two weeks they used two real missiles.

In the meantime the family were resistant due to their anti-Semitic sentiment and the twenty year age difference between the two. Karl Moll barely knew what was going on and was furious with his wife: *We had dodged Klimt, and now comes this one, a liberal. An ugly, old and sick man, full of debts, expelled from the opera and writing works that are not worth anything!* Perfunctory and biased.

The friend Burckhard jealous because he in turn was in love with the beautiful Alma, was less rude but not less perfidious: *Her, a creature so beautiful and from such a good family. It will ruin everything if she marries that degenerated Jew. Think of the children they will have! Nice people would say.* Fortunately Alma shrugged this off and it would take a lot more to stop her.

With Moll and Mahler the two became friends, the stepfather-painter assisted Mahler personally in the last moments of life. He even made and cast his funeral mask. However the anti-Semitism at the Moll household would never cease. The same Karl, in the thirties became a fervent Nazi, together with his young daughter Mary and her husband. The three in a final tragedy, decided to commit suicide the day in which the Soviets occupied Vienna.

The Last Tycoon

Before marriage, Mahler wanted to make it clear that the only composer in the family would be him. He did this by writing a long twenty-two page poem.

Mahler either had the gift of synthesis or had the ability to trace all things in a well-planned program like a complicated construction of a Wagnerian opera. Alma was required with grace to unconditionally surrender. Her parents, and friends advised Alma to immediately break off the engagement. She decided the opposite and with a heavy heart, put on hold her beloved compositions (which will be gloriously reopened almost ten years later by the same Mahler, but that's another story) and accepted the conditions.

Meanwhile during visits to her beautiful home of Moll, Mahler played his music at the piano. One day he played his Fourth symphony and asked his beloved what she thought of it. *The same things written better by Haydn* she replied, causing hilarious laughter from Gustav: *One day you will change your mind!* And then filled with excitement he reached for her mother and shouted: *Mom, after having played, I ask you once again for the hand of your daughter.*

When it came to getting to know Mahler's relatives and friends, there was his sister Justine, who in those days was planning her engagement to the first violinist of the Opera, Arnold Rosé.

There were also a few of Mahler's pre-engagement friends, including Siegfried Lipinier, a poet and playwright who enjoyed the esteem of Wagner and Nietzsche. These just never got along with Alma, Lipinier belittled her calling her a baby. On the first reception with Gustav and Alma, Lipinier was present with his first wife, his second wife and her lover in charge! Bold and brazen. To make things worse that evening there was also the singer Anna Von Mildenburg, former mistress of Gustav. Alma faced the challenge and the question from Mildenburg: *What do you think of the music of Gustav?* She replied: *Of this I know very little, but the little I know I do not like.* Fortunately Mahler resorted to the usual laughter and broke the tense atmosphere.

Alma started making a long list of enemies. However, with her organisational skills and practical sense, most of these turned out to be pretty harmless.

In the presence of many witnesses, the surprise engagement was announced whilst Mahler appeared on the podium of the Opera. He received huge applauses and all the crowd's eyes travelled towards Alma, the unsuspecting girlfriend who wanted to disappear due to her embarrassment.

Such was the emotions and feelings at Felix Vienna!

In one last desperate act to try and stop the marriage from proceeding, Von Mildenburg the day after the announcement rushed to the office of Mahler making incredible scenes followed by the traditional fainting, salts, fainting and again salts.

This was, in a sense, the ultimate romantic attempt to stop the wedding of the century in Vienna. Mahler's friends and former lovers had underestimated the beautiful doe. They all believed that it would be easy to subdue this young girl. They did not factor in the pride and the spirit of independence of Alma.

But it is time for the marriage to proceed.

Marriage and life together

'Wet bride lucky bride', in fact on 9 March 1902 in Vienna it rained. The church which was chosen was the Church of St. Charles Borromeo. A grand and beautiful baroque church, ample enough to accommodate the bridal party of ten people.

The bride and bridegroom, the parents of Alma, Justine and Arnold Rosé (who would marry the next day). At the moment when the bride and groom knelt, Mahler who was unfamiliar with Catholic affairs leaned on

▲ Gustav and Alma in one of their trips, she was the highest and towered above Mahler even more thanks to hats and outfits that only increased and widened ... (Basel 1903)

the floor instead of kneeling. Given that he was small in stature, whilst Alma was a mighty matron by comparison, the extra 15 cm of height made it look like Alma was marrying a dwarf.

It was a riotous scene that made everybody smile including the celebrant. After the ceremony, the bridal party (reduced to six people) went to breakfast and immediately after to Russia, Petrograd the capital. The announcement of the marriage was purposefully misleading as it was announced that the wedding was going to take place in the evening. As a result of this, the curious followers ended up seen nothing.

Last pill of Alma - Alma as composer

Immediately after the drama that developed in the home of Mahler as a result of betrayal of Alma with Walter Gropius, in an attempt to win back his young wife's heart, he threw himself into action and opened the drawer of Alma's old compositions...

He discovered the great compositional value of his wife, and was struggling with the Freudian title: *In meines Vaters Garten* (in my father's garden). Mahler called her with excitement asking Alma: what do you think of a reduction here, a cut there? Do you think this is better?

Whereupon the towering Alma shocked her husband by replying: *Gustav in these matters you are much more skilled!*

New Love

Madam, the thing is this..... Alma's lovers, she almost always choose geniuses and giants of Central European culture who enriched her almost every day. Among the last, even the unsuspected Belgian painter Fernand Khnopff, the mysterious creator of Medusa and sirens with sealed lips.

Even here there is felt the expert but fatal hugs of Alma Mahler. After Mahler, Klimt, Kokoschka, Gropius, Werfel, the Rev. Hollensteiner (in the mould of a cardinal and thirty years younger), but the Belgian Khnopff amongst this listing was indeed a misfit.

Conclusion

I had read several sources of Mahler, and have reflected on Alma. Luckily for me, just recently I have leafed through the pages of the memoirs, records and letters of these two.

The image that emerges of Alma from all these sources is the importance of this woman for art and ultimately to the success of the men who have had the good fortune of meeting her along their journey. However, they struggled to offer effective interpretations about her charm and seductive power. Often we wonder, but what did she have which was so special? This question remains suspended in mid-air whilst we are distracted by the musical brilliance of her husband, the brilliant architecture of her second husband, and the charming writing of her third husband. Or in front of the wonderful paintings of Klimt and Oskar Kokoschka. We get to know her often by indirect means, via what is told by third parties and often in the biographies that are largely devoted to these great men.

The sound of her voice which is often hidden in her memoirs, letters and records often touches the inner feelings of the reader. Alma explains, tells, narrates, describes, her thoughts and is convincing. The men like me are left entirely spellbound and seduced. In short she was a grand woman.

When she died in 1964, she wanted to be buried like the ancient Egyptian pharaohs, with a lot of stuff that could be used in the afterlife. Alongside all the scores of Tristan and Isolde to be ready to be played at the time of the last judgment.

▲ Alma with Franz Werfel her third husband, the writer and Austrian playwright of Jewish origin, author of the famous: "Pale Blue Ink in a Lady's Hand"

▶ Alma with his two daughters had by Mahler: Maria Anna (1902-1907), who died very young of diphtheria, and Anna (1904-1988)

▲ The Mahler spouses on the occasion of one of two trips in Italy. In this image with an Italian friend, the historian Federico Spiro on the Via Appia Antica in Rome.

▶ Alma in all its *"liberty"* splendor in this well-known portrait photos.

MAHLER, THE OTHER WOMEN

"Women do not exist"
Jacques Lacan

Alma was without doubt the most fiery, important and passionate lover in Mahler's life. The major shareholder of Gustav's love life, but Alma was not the only one. Sigmund Freud saw at once the importance that women played in Mahler's life. The great Viennese psychoanalyst after having visited, declared: *the wife Alma loved her father Rudolf Schindler and could only seek and love that kind of man.*
The age of Mahler, with which he had so much fear, was what made him so attractive in his wife's eyes. Mahler in fact loved his mother and always tried to find somebody similar in his women. His mother troubled and full of suffering, unconsciously reappeared in his wife Alma.
So comforted by Freud, we can surmise that the first important woman in his life in every sense was his mother, Marie Hermann. This poor and unhappy woman gave birth to as many as 14 children, most of whom died prematurely.

Of the many brothers, his sister Justine was also a reference point and support during his long years as a bachelor. Please refer to the chapter on Mahler's family for further details. Here we are interested instead in the complex story of all Mahler's women, including Alma. The women that he fell in love, was seduced intrigued and sentimentally involved with Gustav Mahler.
The primary source to which we refer to are the memoirs written by his wife Alma, notes written years after the death of her husband.
It was a known fact that Mahler's widow had an intense and troubled life, both before and after Mahler, and this influenced greatly her writing of her memories. The reports contain information which is clearly in part diluted, partly sweetened, and very often missing. Surprisingly, at least in the early edition of these memories, they are not her letters to Gustav, but rather his letters to her, and this group was appropriately selected and vetted.
In telling the tragic events of the turbulent summer of 1910 in Dobbiaco, one of the main protagonists of that sort of Wagnerian tragedy was Walter Gropius (then lover and later second husband of Alma) is ridiculously referred to by the badly conceal identity of a capital X.
So in accordance with the most renowned musicologists and also with the thoughts of the most important Mahlerian biographer Henry

▲ The brothers Gustav and Justine Mahler. Of all his brothers Justine was the closest to the great composer, sometimes too much.
▶ The Soldar-Roger quartet with violinist Natalie Bauer-Lechner, a great friend of Mahler (second from right).

Louis de la Grange, even I invite you to consider carefully the memories of his wife Alma, which ultimately brings us a picture of the composer like an ascetic chaste, a person with few and insignificant romances apart from the passionate relationship with Alma.

The first to argue this data was Mahler himself, who in a lengthy written correspondence during the time of their engagement tells her: *I offered you without any defence totally my heart, I have dedicated my entire life to you, I have not known young ladies or rich, beautiful, educated, young women etc.*

The reality was somewhat different, and new revelations reveal that he in fact had many relationships and infatuations.

Among the latest reliable sources on the real amorous experience of Mahler was a short letter with the significant title of: *Brief BER Mahler Lieben* (Letter on Mahler's lovers) written by his confidante (and lover), the violinist Natalie Bauer - Lechner, also the author of a journal devoted to her friendship with Mahler.

We start with this very famous violinist. Natalie knew Mahler in 1890. At the time, she was

the violin player of a famous all female string quartet, Soldat - Roger. The two musicians spoke the same language, touched the same chords, and by 1902 they had a constant and intense partnership. A woman of character, idealistic, and a feminist, Natalie was born in 1858, two years before Mahler.

Their first meeting took place in the halls of the Vienna Conservatory but was not decisive. It was in fact only in 1890, after the failure of the violist's marriage that the two started dating. She was presented to his family and she accompanied Mahler on his alpine walks. She organised dinners, listen to him and spent time beside him.

These were very important years for the creativity of Gustav, increasingly become more famous as a conductor, from the Hamburg Opera to the glorious seasons at the Theatre of the Vienna Court.

Natalie is always nearby, generous with useful advice. Meanwhile, she memorised everything, his reflections, ideas and thoughts that fed Mahler's music and the pillars of classical music: Beethoven, Bach, Liszt, and Wagner. She assisted in dialogues with the great musicians still living, or his contemporaries such as Brahms, Strauss and Debussy.

She understood his genius, greatness and strength. From her vantage point we have an insight into their love hate relationship which was typical among many musicians and singers, but this great man, thanks to his interpretative genius raised huge applause at every exhibition he brought to Vienna the likes of which was not seen again. Years later Mahler died, Natalie ordered all her notes and transformed them into a work with an explicit title. These notes outline their relationship, and are full of anecdotes and curiosity about the musician and the musical life of that era.

Natalie also had the good fortune to witness the genesis of his first symphonies and the first Lieder from *Des Knaben Wunderhorn* onwards, which she recounts in her pages.

Unfortunately, the open nature and philanthropy of the amateur violist does not help to ensure the integrity of this diary.

Often she would lend her diary to her friends and co-workers with the result that sometimes some pages have disappeared, and day after day this precious document thinned more and more. What is left of this diary is now the property of the Parisian foundation of Henry - Louis de La Grange. Fortunately some excerpts of the original appeared in some newspapers of the time, in 1913 and in 1920 following the death of Bauer - Lechner, but for thereafter nobody cared about these.

These memories are in fact amongst the most important primary sources for the understanding of Mahler, especially with regard to his previous marriage with Alma. Natalie was a musician and had a perceptive musical mind. This is why Mahler took her seriously, and for this reason this resource has so much value. News and memories that were saved from the censorship that the widow of Mahler consciously or not excised for life to protect her husband's image, in what the Mahler scholars appropriately define the problem, Alma.

Very intuitive, Natalie concluded: *A month and a half ago Mahler is engaged to Alma Schindler. I would find myself in the position of a doctor forced to treat the person most dear to me while he struggles between life and death. I entrust his fate in the hands of the eternal and supreme Master!*

But let's leave Natalie to her justified and understandable discouragement, and return to the account of his unpublished letter the Brief *BER Mahler Lieben*. As mentioned it is a quick but comprehensive overview of all the amorous adventures experienced by Mahler starting from the years in Jglau and ending with the arrival of Alma in his life.

It starts with Josephine Poisl, the daughter of a postman of Jglau, where Mahler had moved since 1861, and the place where Gustav grew up and lived his youth.

The story of Josephine dates back to the years 1877 to 1880. Mahler was finishing his final year at the Vienna Conservatory, which he joined in 1875.

His love for Josephine will be the baptism to his first published work: *i Das Lied klagende* (the song of lament) which in fact was completed in 1880. In addition to the music, the lyrics are entirely those of the author. Always for the same beloved he realized three other musical works, the *lied: Im Lenz, Winterlied* and *Maitanz im grnen* (1880). The fact that the romance ended shortly after the completion of the third lied is the reason behind its incompleteness which was meant to have five lieds.

▲ The singer Marie Gutheil-Schoder at left, and on the right the beautiful Selma Kurz.
◄ A well-known portrait of the violinist Natalie Bauer-Lechner.

After his love with the commoner Jglau, he begins his long affairs with sopranos, half sopranos or women related to music. Among them one remembers the singers Margarethe Michalek, Johanna Richter, Selma Kurz and Anna von Mildenburg.

Michalek is known for being the first star of the second symphony, as well as having appeared in numerous other Mahler operas. Johanna Richter, a dramatic soprano met Mahler in 1884 when he held the post of Meister Kappell at Kassel and she was the dedicatee of the *Gesellen lied* (the wanderer singing), or rather to be precise, these lieder were written just at the end of their very passionate and stormy love affair. In fact, this is realized in the Schubert lieder that tells a story in which their affair is a mixture of love and renunciation.

There is more information on Selma Kurz, a beautiful woman, fragile and delicate. She was from a Jewish family like Mahler, the soprano met Mahler at the time when she was already the music director of the Vienna Opera.

He had heard her sing in Frankfurt near the end of 1898, he was impressed and asked her to audition for him. This fact helped cement her ultimate success as a singer which lasted until the end of her musical career, thirty years later. Mahler immediately assigned her the role of absolute prima donna. The two ended up falling in love and had a brief affair during the spring of 1900. However, the Court Opera in Vienna, by statute, curiously did not allow its members to marry each other, and Selma would not give up her career preferring then to end their relationship.

A curious posthumous epilogue tells us that the love was still simmering in the embers long after it was ended, thus providing a confirmation to the romance between the two.

1910 in Dobbiaco, Mahler was in the habit of inviting friends and various guests together. Among these he had a visit from Kurz, who had the misfortune to meet on that occasion some guests of Alma, who were persistent gossips about the old love affair she had with Mahler.

The singer at one point angrily jumped up. She made rude gestures towards these people commenting loudly: *There are many pigs in Vienna, and I have the impression that there are some even among us.*

Another very important love for Mahler was the singer Anna von Mildenburg (curiously the Bauer - Lechner wrote in her diary that Mildenburg confided in her one day that the nature of this love was purely platonic). Mahler first met Mildenburg at an audition for the Valkyries in 1895 in Hamburg.

Ever since that first meeting, the emotions born between the two were obvious. Soon came the exchange of letters, books and small gifts, but always in a strange amorous way, complicated and often stressful.

The capricious and fickle character of the hysterical Mildenburg put a strain on the psyche and the patience of Mahler. The abandonment of his musical direction in Hamburg was greeted with relief as this allowed him to put a healthy end to this passion, even though the singer later chose to follow Mahler to Vienna.

Meanwhile the rumours and accusations grew mainly amongst females which referred to the singer as a social climber, always looking for relationships with powerful and wealthy men. These rumours determined once and for all the complete and total closure of their relationship, as evidenced by a curious letter from Mahler (recently sold at an auction), which announced the end of this relationship with irate statements.

Loving each other passionately was of great

▲ The soprano Anna von Mildenburg, certainly among the most famous and important women in the life of Mahler, tried in every way to restrain the wedding of his beloved with Alma.

▶ Always Anna von Mildenburg with her husband, the author and screenwriter Hermann Bahr.

importance, similar to what would occur years later in the relationship between Gustav and Alma. This great singer however remained protective of Mahler, and he reserved the most significant parts of the preparations of Wagner's Ring for her.

There were similarities between Mildenburg and Alma, so much so that they were often confused in photos in which they appear in Mahler's company. The most famous of these photos is the one that shows Mahler together with Alma in a Dobbiaco pasture. A few sources state that the woman in the photo is Von Mildenburg, and the setting is the meadows of Carinthia.

Alma in her memoirs, while reiterating the concept of being almost asexual, often expressed open jealousy when it came to matters between her husband and Mildenburg, she ignominiously referred to her as Madam M. She also made appearance where ever they moved to, in Vienna, in various theatres around Europe and even in Maiernigg.

Less clear is his relationships with the other singers like Sophie Sedlmair or Marie Gutheil - Schoder, Weimar soprano called to Vienna by Gustav Mahler, who bluntly called her a genius. Among the most important of the pre-Alma relationships would certainly be the one which elapsed with Marion Mathilde von Weber, born in Schwabe Manchester in 1856, probably of a Jewish family.

In Leipzig, Marion was the wife of the nephew of the famous composer Carl Maria von Weber. The husband was a Saxon army officer and the couple had three children. Marion was a very passionate woman and she consumed Mahler completely. Curiously the opportunity that favoured the approach was for professional reasons. Her husband Karl Von Weber took advantage of the presence of the celebrated director in the city

and provided him with a very difficult task. The re-reading and possibly the completion of a comic opera of one of his famous ancestor of the same name: the *Drei Pintos.*

Mahler at the beginning, just peeking at the booklet was taken by anxiety and wanted to decline the engagement. The missing parts were too numerous, and what was present was not in the least bit understandable. However, one day he had a surge of inspiration and very quickly decrypted the text and was able to complete the work. A work that nevertheless suffered inevitable criticism, the first by Richard Strauss anchíegli in Leipzig at that time. The criticism was essentially that he had developed a mixture of Weberian material with that of Mahler, a similar criticism which occurred several years later to Mahler's Tenth Symphony, as observed by Deryck Cook and other musicologists.

The fact was that Mahler had access to Weber and had freedom to come and go in his home. A similar thing occurred some years later between the Prague teacher and pupil Alban Berg with Hanna Fuchs - Robettin.

These were the years of the genesis of the Symphony No. two, Resurrection. In 1888, Mahler had just started writing this impressive symphony, when in fact he had a grandeous love affair with Marion and the second symphony was completed only for the first movement. For four years thereafter, Mahler did not compose anything else and this says a lot about the amorous involvement of the two.

At the apex of their relationship, the couple decided to confess to her husband. They faced Von Weber together and confessed their love. He made no resistance, but using various arguments evidently succeeded to convince his wife to never see the fiery young composer again. Dazed he left the home of Von Weber at Leipzig and moved away to Prague. However, confidence in the agreement secretly harboured with Marion, she promised to join him in Tutzing on Starnberg, near Monaco.

But Marion did not honour this agreement and in the end she decided to stay with her husband. It is ironic that a similar thing would happen to Mahler years later but in reverse with the other protagonists: Alma and Walter Gropius. A kind of repayment with the same coin.

Thus began Mahler's long period of depression which caused his longest creative break. He took up paper and pen again in 1892 to create *Des Knaben Wunderhorn* Lieder cycle. And finally only in 1893 he took up the drafting of the Second Symphony to bring it finally to completion the following year. The first movement, written during the affair with Marion, with his final *Totenfeier* (funeral) reflected in all its drama the pains and sufferings for the love lost with women.

The years that followed were those that potentially offered more chances at friendship, for example with Natalie

▲ Gustav Mahler with his sister Justine and some friends in Reinchenhall in 1892.
◄ Photo portrait of the singer Margarethe Michalek.

Bauer - Lechner. She was the one who gave back confidence to Gustav, managing to make him start creating music again. But let this be summarised by his own words: *Whilst I was a recluse and isolated from the world in my small room, in Scheherazade until dawn, I regretted my whole life the one in front of the other without declaration, questions and ratings, our psyche and our bodies fused.*
Interesting at this point was the observation Alma made about Bauer - Lechner: *Mrs. B, a friend who was in love with Mahler, and that, however ugly and old, aspired to be the unrequited love. Poisonous as ever!*

Finally a few words about Justine, the beloved sister, discreet companion but constantly present during the years of his bachelorship. Natalie had the misfortune not to be in tune with Justine, defined by her jealous and possessive stance for her brother. It went better for Alma due to the fact that as the romance started with Mahler, Justine started a relationship with the opera violinist Arnold Rosé. Blessed timing, given that Justine married the day after Gustav's wedding. Just in time to let the house of Mahler in Auenbruggergasse become the love nest of the newly married couples of who the whole of Vienna spoke about.

MAHLER ON THE FREUD'S COUCH

"A man who doubts his own love, indeed must, doubt everything else. Inevitably all great men retain something infantile."
Sigmund Freud

Joyful apocalypse, this is the term used by Hermann Broch, a well known Austrian playwright, to describe the state of the art and social life in Vienna. In short, joyous was the air that one breathed in Vienna during those magical years, in which, like an honour, the Austrian capital was referred to as Vienna Felix.
Gay, carefree, ironic, refined and also subtly erotic, Vienna had it all. The best place in the world to live, at the turn of the end 18th and 19th centuries.
Even the great French artist Rodin remained fascinated with Vienna and during his visit in 1902 asked: *The climate, the music and above all the women here everything is beautiful, carefree joyously, but why?*

▲ Vienna at the beginning of XXth cent. is the world capital of culture, the best place to live !!
◄ Gustav Mahler Photography in the Netherlands.

Replied his friend Klimt: *Dear Auguste this is Austria!*

The Habsburgs reigned uninterruptedly for centuries, at the head of a diverse and cosmopolitan population of Bohemians, Germans, Moravians, Hungarians, Bosnians, Galician, Italian, Croats, Slovaks and Jews. The latter were now very well integrated, especially after the Act of Emancipation signed in 1867. Furthermore Francesco Giuseppe hated anti-Semitism.

Here they coexisted, each maintaining their own privileges and separated positions from the aristocracy and the upper middle class. And then there was the art, which in Vienna always had a special place, such as the Imperial Opera royal box. There is no capital, not even Paris where an aestheticism push was cultivated. While in the French capital Hoffmann created his network of boulevards, Vienna drew the tricks along the Ring, the ring that ran along the perimeter of the city where the original walls that defended the city from the Turks in 1683 once where.

It is here where Jugendstil produced its best fruits. The artists of the so-called Secession had their base here. People like Karl Moll (Alma's stepfather), Gustav Klimt, Josef Hoffmann, Otto Wagner and Kolo Moser. And then there was the music. In Vienna at that time people did not frown if you said you wanted to become a musician.

And being a woman in this paradise nestled on the beautiful blue Danube, how was it like? A fortune! It was like being in France at the end of the XVIII century when social and also political courtesans were the crux of the skein. The best salons/lounges in the city were run by women, like the famous one run by Berta Zuckerkandl and it is no coincidence that it is in one of her receptions that the affair between Alma and Gustav was born.

Women in Vienna were casual. Strolling alone, smoking, careless with awkward smiles, riding awkwardly on bicycles and scampering to learn painting, architecture and music.

This is what Alma did, but she was not the only one. However some secular puritanists are die hards. The honour of women was still very important. Every girl wanted to and had to reach their wedding as virgins. If they did not, some conformists thought, there would be a riot, a crescendo of organisms triggered by uncontrollable lust and pleasure.

There was an abundance of topics for the father of psychoanalysis, but also for those who were inquiring about the dark depths of the mind. And indeed in 1903, a young twenty year old, Jewish philosopher Otto Weininger published a study entitled: *Geshlecht und Charakter* (sex and character).

Today these works are considered as sexist, homophobic and anti-Semitic especially in the academic environment. However, the book is filled with interesting insights and quotes that indicate that the dual presence of women and men are in every being.

▲ Sigmund Freud photographed by Max Halberstadt (1922) for the New York Times,
◄ Berta Zuckerkandl (1864-1945), Queen of the Viennese salons.

Weininger had apart from his indisputable virtues, good ears and heard many speeches from people like Freud, Breuer and Jung that indeed disputed the origins of such discoveries. He opened the castle with a stolen key commented Freud. Soon after, maybe due to remorse, the unstable key thief took his own life leaving a note where instead of saying goodbye to loved ones and friends, he announced his irreducible presumption of his spiritual testament: *I think I have given a definitive answer to what is known as women's issues. A late romantic spirit one cannot say.*

Meanwhile, however, the stone was thrown in the pond, and in the words of Freud now finally we can say that: *I am no longer master in my own home.* The Viennese cultured, intellectuals, and all those who made sufficient use of the brain were adapted quickly to these new philosophies of modern thought. However many loved lingering in the contradiction that traditionally formed in the middle.

Arthur Schnitzler is a case in point, Freud himself highly regarded Arthur's brain, who liked to quip: *What I would love the best is a harem and I would not like to be disturbed!*

At first it seemed that even the Herr Direktor of the Vienna Opera, took up this matter, and in one of the first letters he wrote to Alma during the engagement, he wrote: *Dear Alma do not think that during the relationship between husband and wife, I think of my wife as a sort of hobby, dedicated to domestic chores and her husband's service. Do not think that I have these thoughts?*

Mahler is keen to make a good impression, and certainly said what he thought. But this extraordinary complex personality, the culture in which he soaked in and was born in, led him to ask for even more control of his future wife. This was included in a very heavy and complete historical letter of about twenty-two pages. This view was hard to bear for any woman let alone the rebellious spirit of Alma Schindler. An attitude probably typical of geniuses, which just cannot help but to act like this, as they are assured of having an inwardly divine mission, that higher fate has chosen them and not others.

The additional problem in this specific pair is that Alma, which everyone understands and realizes, in this case does not grasp fully the genius of Mahler and does not particularly like the music. Moreover, to contradict many of the choices she will make in her life, Alma is anti-Semitic, steeped in Nietzschean theories, radically misunderstood, brainwashed by her tutor, Max Burckhard, the great Viennese theatre man, 25 years older

▲ The Mahler house of Maiernigg on the Wörthersee, a small lake in Carinthia.
◀ Portrait of Gustav Mahler.

than her, hopelessly in love with the young girl and therefore jealous of the Jew Mahler.
He transmitted to the girls his love for the music of Schubert, Beethoven and Wagner, but absurdly little consideration for the Italian music. Furthermore, it is filled with pseudo-scientific concepts to demonstrate that Jews could not aspire to be creative.
In some ways, the strong attraction of Alma for Mahler was conformist. She was struck by the great conductor, the aura that surrounded him, and by his success. In short, there was already a germ of some secure but complicated future between the two even before the two commenced their courting.
In fact, the first signs of unhappiness and depression which arrived, was known by a very evocative and romantic name, *obscure melancholy*.
Even in the early months of their marriage, Alma felt caged: *I have a feeling that I have had my wings clipped. Gustav, why did you want to capture this magnificent bird, happy to fly, while for you, you would be more suitable with a grey and heavy bird.*
She lacked everything, she missed her friends, especially those in Vienna, from where she had to move away from for long periods of time in order to follow the creative Mahler to his beautiful villa on Maiernigg Wrthersee in Carinthia: *I had to lose all my friends in order to find one who does not even know me.*
She lived through two pregnancies and two miscarriages, both very painful, but she soon found herself with two wonderful daughters, having to deal with them without having any maternal instincts. Gustav lived his life. *My daughter does not need me. And I cannot continue to deal with her exclusively.*
Mahler at first does not understand, he then realises but does not know which way to turn. He decided to do what he does best, he writes her a beautiful and poignant lied: *Liebst du um Schnheit* (If you love for beauty) which forms part of *R ckert lied*. He hide the sheet music on Alma's grand piano pretending nothing of it and when she found it, it would be a moment of high emotion, but soon everything returned back to what it was before.

▲ family photos in the Maiernigg villa with the two children. It was a happy time for Mahler, who composed in those summers several symphonies and lieder cycles, alternating between swimming in the lake. While Alma darkening increasingly feeling the futility of a life to do just as mother and wife, killing its large youthful aspirations ..

▶ Even the two children along with a housekeeper. The sudden death of Anna Maria will change cards on the table.

Meanwhile Alma was not feeling well. Their mutual friend Bruno Walter, Mahler's assistant director at the Opera, who recovered from a similar depression advised her of a good Viennese doctor, namely Sigmund Freud, who helped him to recover. His recovery was after Walter had tried everything like therapies sludge, magnetism, concoctions and various wizardry.

Alma forgets for the moment this suggestion, but will remember it later, but meanwhile time passes.

1907 proved to be a terrible year. The situation of Mahler at the Vienna State Opera became unsustainable, continuing tensions led him at last to offer his resignation. However, he already had a safety net in his pocket, it was a generous four-year contract with the New York Metropolitan. Mahler moved overseas and stayed there for three months a year overseas. The hope was that even their problems would take a break. Tragedy instead knocked relentlessly at their door. The family retired to Maiernigg to spend one last summer in peace after the tumultuous months of the resignation, witnessing the drama of their first daughter's illness: Anna Maria Putzi. Putzi barely had six years and had a bad diphtheria likened to scarlet fever. Putzi struggled for two weeks with this illness until the 12 July when her little heart gave in. The parents were destroyed, and the remaining sister who lived beyond 80 years would always feel guilty for the rest of her life.

The Mahlers left their villa in Maiernigg never to return, and soon the villa would be sold. Some time later they elected to vacate at a large home in Dobbiaco in the Puster valley where they divided their time between there and Vienna during the months when Gustav was not engaged at the Metropolitan.

Time passed and the reputation of Mahler continued to grow and reached its peak. The years at Dobbiaco and New York saw the birth of the last three symphonies including *Das Liede von der Erde,* true symphony of lied. But the master was a little superstitious, and decided not to chose for this masterpiece the title of the ninth symphony, which statistically is for many composers their last, for example with Beethoven and Bruckner. For Mahler he composed another ninth and also a piece of the tenth symphony. Alma, would continue to deteriorate and visited many doctors, but not the ones that could help her.

The worthy doctors advised her to cure her frayed nerves by bathing in good spa water. This did help cure her, but it was luck which led her to choose this mediocre treatment.

The Tobelbad spa in Styria was chosen. Alma and Gustav had been married for seven years, and as a whole it can be said that in 1910 their marriage was beginning to move towards a relative stable condition.

He became less demanding and more understanding, although he never knew when to give up the spirit of complete abnegation for his Alma, formulated in his famous letter of twenty-two pages.

She for her part seemed to enter into a quieter period of her life. And in a sense he was resigned to this and indulged her, but his unconscious continued to knock on the door, or rather to put it in a clearer imagery, he was just knocking out the door!

And the responsibility for these domestic destruction, already in the antechamber of Dobbiaco farm was the one who in fact was able to build a home second to none.

Alma, with interest and active cooperation from her mother (the ambiguous Anna Moll) met at the spa a young handsome and good-looking man, a German, in fact a Prussian. Obviously he was not an ordinary man. Alma had a special eye for these things as some dogs have for truffles, she did not miss a beat. Her new superman was Walter Gropius, the future director of the Bauhaus and destined to become alongside Le Corbusier and F.L.Wright one of the most important architects of all time. But at the time, he was above all lost in the grace and beauty of Alma.

At Tobelbad there grew an intensely addictive love which did not give up anything, favoured and supported by her mother, who as an experienced woman clearly knew what her daughter needed to cure her nerves.

The cure however ended and Mahler, at Dobbiaco becomes increasingly restless for his young wife who was behaving strangely and did not even find the time to write to him. Alma then re-joined her husband in the Puster valley, still oblivious to everything. The two lovers meanwhile continued to write to each other in daring and fiery text in secret.

Until one day an interesting thing happened. One of the many letters that Gropius wrote to Alma and like the others, full of impatient invocations and promises of love, for some reason the recipient's name on the envelope was recorded as Mr Director Mahler.

▲ Mahler at his work table, he was in a similar situation who found the letter of Walter Gropius.
▶ Above the hotel Schwarzer Adler (Black Eagle) in Dobbiaco where the young architect Walter Gropius spent the night and where later he was joined by Alma. Below the Dobbiaco Train Station, which represented the last leave of the passionate lover, that only years later will become the second husband of Alma. (Author's photo)

The reason for this apparent confusion will never be disclosed nor explained. It was noted that Gropius had a strange and unpleasant propensity for trying to seduce married women whose husbands in turn somehow seduced Gropius' mind due to the fascination Gropius had with the status of these husbands or composers.
Meantime, a letter arrived and was leaning on the piano on the first floor of the house at Trenker at Dobbiaco. Mahler returning from his composition cottage in the forest, saw it, opened it and read it.
He then called Alma and asked her: *What is this thing here?* Alma in turn read the letter and here explodes the tragedy. With controlled voice she confessed everything, and seemed liberated in doing so. An outlet for well over seven years: *Finally I could tell him everything!* She commented years later.
Mahler not defied did not scream nor did he reproach her. Simply he felt like dying inside. He felt that the world had collapsed around him. For some reason she tried to tranquilize him and informed him immediately that she will not abandon him. They talk for hours, always in low tones, then Mahler exhausted called to his aid the guilty mother-in-law.
His devastation was complete. At night, he silently stood in front of the bed where Alma slept, when she woke she was frightened at seen a sort of ghost that looked desperate. During the day, he was consumed with crying continuously in his composition shed.
But this Greek type tragedy was still missing a finale.
A few days after the reading of this letter, at Dobbiaco Gropius arrived. Alma had instructed him to stay

away, but the youth madly in love refused to listen to reason. Gropius began to stake out the home of Mahler, until eventually late one evening, while the couple were outside the house they noticed a person hidden under the nearby railway bridge. Alma immediately understood who it was, but it was Mahler who took charge of the matter. He reached Gropius and invited him to follow him to the house under a dim light of a candle in a sort of decadent pre-Raphaelite picture.

He left the two lovers in the lounge and retired to his room to read the Bible. But Alma lingered only a few moments with her lover and re-joined the preoccupied Mahler in his room. He was shaken but found the strength to whisper: *Do what you feel comfortable doing, what you do will be well done. You need to make your choice.*

She went back to Gropius who begged her to leave with him. Alma froze and did not say anything. She remained with her husband. And then once again Mahler accompanied the young man by candle light to the country road. Later Gropius thanked Mahler for his kindness.

The next day, Alma re-joined Gropius for a final farewell, probably they flirted in the Black Eagle hotel room and finally he embarked on the train, Amen!

This then started or rather continued to reinforce the painful torment for poor Gustav, which was written down on the manuscript of his unfinished tenth symphony the following sentences: *Oh God, Oh God, why have you abandoned me.* And once again: *Farewell My lira..I live for you! For you die Almschi!*

The resulting physiological suffering and subsequent humiliation made Mahler become impotent and helpless. It was time to reach out to another superhuman for help: Sigmund Freud.

She recounted to Gustav the experience of Bruno Walter. The facts are interesting and worth recounting. In 1904 Walter had encountered a kind of block to his right limb which meant he was unable to conduct an orchestra, a sort of strange paralysis, almost certainly caused by a nervous shock as a result of attacks from the critics to his work, similar attacks which hit Mahler.

He turned to Freud. The psychoanalyst instead of inquiring into Walter's life (as he would have expected), he asked suddenly if he had ever been

▲ The farm leased by Mahler in Dobbiaco is now the destination of all the Mahler newbies who come here from all over the world. The family occupied the entire first floor where there is a veranda with flowers

▶ Above Gustav Mahler and his daughter Anna in the barn of their house. Great walker, Puster Valley was the perfect place for his walks in the middle of magnificent mountains.

▶ View of Dobbiaco (Toblach) in 1909, precisely the years in which Mahler attended this location.

to Sicily, and with a negative reply, he suggested that he leave as soon as possible to the island. Walter obeyed, visited Sicily and fell in love, but on his return to Vienna his arm was still paralysed. He then went back to Freud to ask for an explanation. Freud then ordered him to resume the treatment and managed to convince him to attend six sessions. The prescription of Freud's work, namely sending Walter to Sicily had nothing to do with psychoanalysis. It appeared that Freud had realized immediately in the young, educated and intelligent patient what his symptom was. Therefore sending him to the ancient empire probably meant that Freud had no spare time at that point to treat him. For Freud, Greece (where he had recently visited with much enthusiasm) and Sicily were intimately connected. The invitation to visit Sicily therefore was to go back to his childhood to seek the origin of the prohibitions that prevented success.

But now it was Mahler's turn, except Freud was not in Vienna, but on holiday in Leiden in the Netherlands with two of his sons. Fortunately, due to Alma's connections, she knew a cousin Nepallek who was a neurologist and they tried to arrange an appointment for the illustrious patient.

For his first engagement, Mahler made raving notes in a continuous stream and left these at the bedside table of his wife. *Source of my life, I have kissed a thousand times your little slippers, and I stopped, full of longing near your doorstep, the demons have punished me a thousand times over because I thought of myself and not of you.*

And yet, with the illusion of surprise he throws himself into the lieder written by his wife, which he always considered to be mediocre. Now he gets excited to read them, he played the piano for hours as he had never done before and considered her work as a wonder and as a star that will always shed light on his firmament

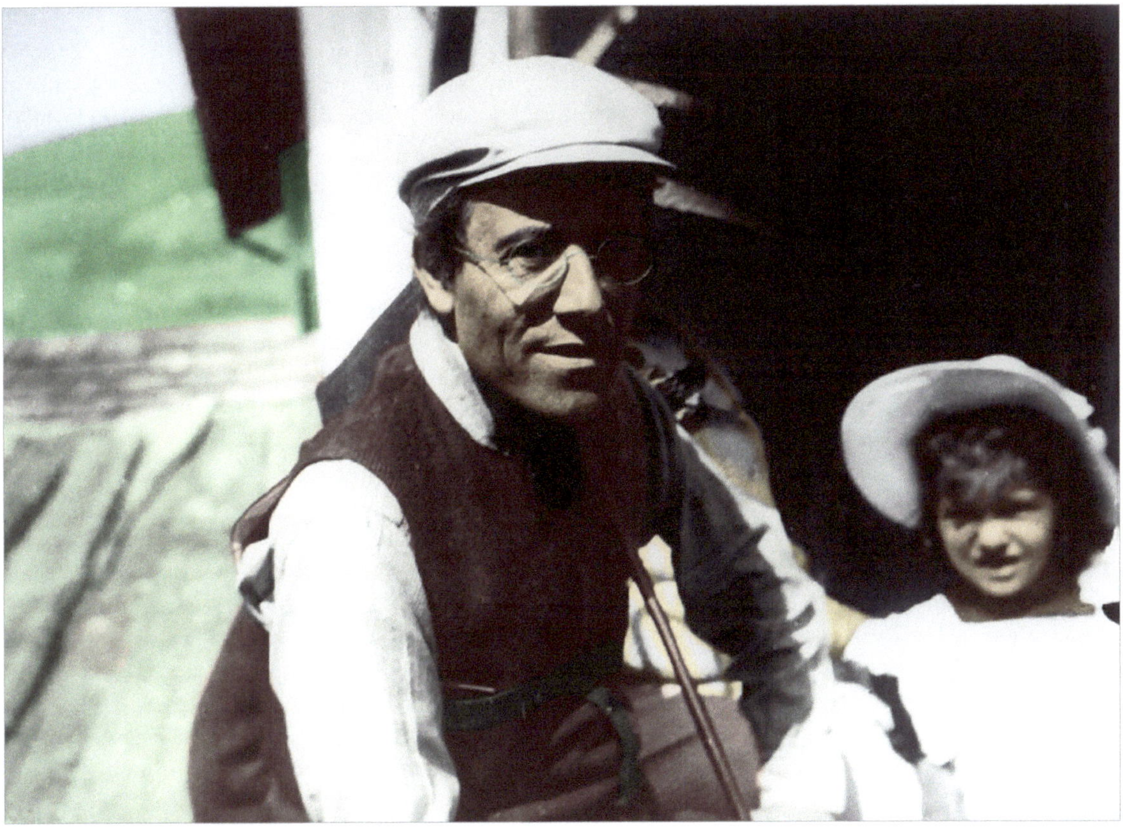

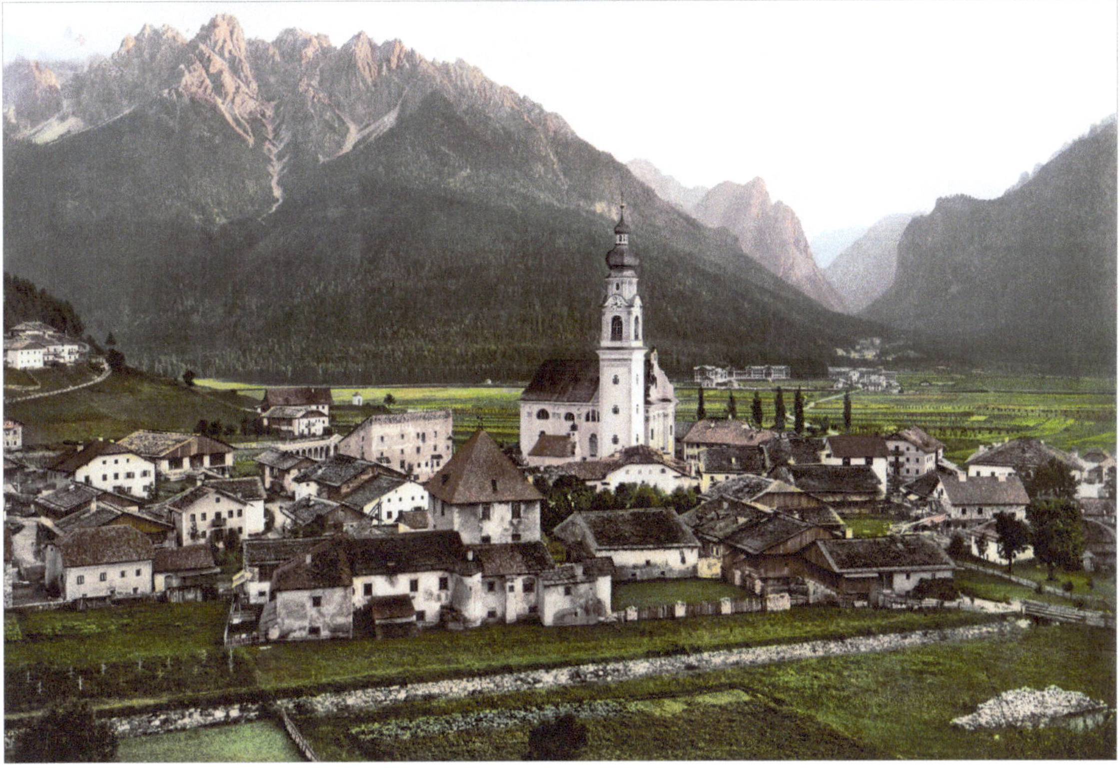

(sic).

As with an hourglass when the dust ends, the dominance in the relationship between the two now changed. It is no longer he who dominates her, but the exact opposite. Years after, Mahler's widow, with treacherous coquetry, will frame these notes in the living room of her Viennese house, like a prestigious hunting trophy but also as a warning to prospective suitors.

Alma is a kind of Turandot revisited? Freud gets to work. The great doctor was organizing his coveted trip to Sicily, but agreed nonetheless to see Mahler who was in the throes of a full-bodied obsessional malaise. It must be said that Freud saw this as an opportunity and admitted: *to know all the psychological understanding of an extraordinary creative genius.*

However, for various reasons, on this occasion he could not achieve what he could with Walter. Mahler had a certain amount of innate resistance to psychoanalytic therapy and viewed science as a dark object. With Walter he had time and also the strategy of the Sicilian trip, and he was left with a far more docile patient. This was not the case with Mahler and everything was forcibly condensed into four hours of chatting along the canals of Leiden in the Netherlands.

Freud felt or guessed that there would be space and time for further effective therapy, but in fact Mahler survived less than a year after the visit at the end of August 1910.

Meanwhile, as expected the patient did resist. He sent a telegram to Freud to request a meeting, and soon after he sent a second one cancelling the appointment. A few days after, this scene repeated itself: a new appointment followed by a cancellation. With the third booking and cancellation, Freud decided to take charge of the situation and put Mahler's back to the wall and informed him that he did not have much more time left. Freud was aware of the clinical symptoms affecting Mahler and was not surprised. He retold this fact years later to Ernest Jones, his biographer, he said that Mahler suffered from folie de doute (madness of doubt) caused by his obsessional neurosis, and that this explained his indecisions. Mahler then suspended his work on the 10th symphony and with four traumatic round trips, Mahler finally met Freud in Leyden. The

▲ Three generations of women and ten husbands and an even larger number of lovers!
Alma, with his daughter Anna (*Gucki*) and mother Anna Moll photographed here with Mahler, the half-sister Maria Moll and his friend and colleague Oskar Fried on Lake Braies platform (Prager Wildsee) at Dobbiaco 1910. Maria Moll and her Karl's father years later will become fervent Nazi, and will be featured in an expropriation of their own works of art to the detriment of Alma Mahler, who as the wife of Mahler first and then the writer Franz Werfel jew had to flee Austria. The photo is very important as it was taken immediately after the famous Mahler-Gropius Crisis.

meeting between the two took place during the weekend of 26 and 27 August 1910.

The story of what was said in that short time span lies in the memories of Freud himself and recounted in his biography. The meeting had the merit of calming Mahler a little. The musician obviously had not, as almost all the people of that time, any knowledge of psychoanalysis, so many theorems must have seemed very strange. But when Freud accidentally discovered a nominal link between his mother Maria and wife Alma, this reignited his interest.

The doctor confirmed that his attitude and his neuroses could be seen in some way as a way to re-establish his instinctive need to see the woman who lived next door, the

▶ The composition hut in Dobbiaco, here in a drawing stepfather of Alma, Karl Moll.

◀ The pier on Lake Braies (Pragser Wildsee) as it is today. Is virtually the same as when they sat in the Mahler picture above on this page.

mother figure. The mother Maria was an unhappy bride, distressed by the fact that eight of her fourteen off springs died prematurely, she led a very poor and wretched life.

To see his mother once again, he needed Alma to suffer. But there are considerations for Alma.

Freud ruled that Alma by marrying a short, wise and far older man in Mahler, actually was looking for a man who reminded her of her father. A father who Alma adored (to whom she dedicated one of her most successful lied: *In meines Vaters Garten*). So at least for this fact, Mahler who always considered her to be a mess, gave him peace. The age difference is not the problem, since this is the main reason why Alma was attracted to him.

On the way back, Mahler took advantage of all the railway stations to send reassuring telegrams to his wife. But back to the meeting, or better yet the walk at Leiden. In the memories assigned by the father of psychoanalysis to his disciple Marie Bonaparte, there is also an interesting theorem relating to music, of which Freud is not the least passionate. He recalled that in a passage Mahler confided his inability on his part to reach high levels in his music.

It was as if there was some sort of internal appeal, a bell that at some point summoned him to order, forcing him to insert a trivial melody in the work. And in fact, many of the works of Mahler, especially his Fifth Symphony, has these dual characteristic.

At times there are high intimate lyricism as in the case of the fifth, the famous *adagietto* (but also the first movement *Trauermarsch*), interspersed with lighter and gay tones. Various musicologists and critics have always pointed out and identified in Mahler's music the presence of songs relating to his childhood. Arising from the memory of military marches, funerals or simply passing orchestras. The recognition of these supposedly weak or mediocre musical pieces by the same author was for the first time told during the Leiden dialogue. Continuing his story he told Freud, always in relation to his music, Mahler recounted a violent scene which he witnessed as a child.

He told that his father, who was a rather rough and brutal individual, one day beat his poor wife. The young Gustav, scared and shaken fled from this tragic scene unable to tolerate it. He found himself in the great square of Iglau, where he heard the sound of one of those vertical accordions who passed through the countryside, which was playing a popular Viennese song: *O du lieber Augustin!* Listening to this tune had the benefit of calming the boy's mind a little to what he had just experienced.

Freud came to the conclusion that Mahler had an innate need to blend the highs and lows in his music, just as had happened in his own life. Curiously, this need to combine the

tragic with the gay returned also in other situations.

For example, when Mahler decided to devote himself to the writing of *Kindertotenlieder* (songs for the dead children) at Maiernigg, the very years that his two daughters were born, with ample disgust from Alma who just failed to understand him. A strange mixture of happiness given to him by the birth of his daughters had to be compensated by the memory of severe pain at the loss of so many of his brothers who died at an early age.

At the end of it Freud confided to his colleague Theodor Reik, who was a fanatic Mahlerian, the following: *I analysed Mahler and if I am to believe what has been written, I have had some success with him. He asked my opinion as to why his wife had risen after he had fallen which was the story of his life, I analysed his sexual behaviour and, above all, his Oedipus complex. I also had several opportunities to learn about the deep psychological penetration capacity of this brilliant man. It was not however possible to shed light on the symptomatic aspects of his obsessional neurosis. It was as if he had dug a deep narrow well in a mysterious building.*

So even the great doctor realized that his subject was a tough cookie. However as mentioned above, the patient returned in a little better frame of mind, even though four hours of analysis, albeit with the father of psychoanalysis could not work miracles.

He finally reached Dobbiaco and Alma. His libido was finally back in operation. Now he can (and does) make love once again with the coveted leading lady in

▲ One of the last pictures of Gustav Mahler, already visibly tried by illness, on board of the transatlantic that brought him back to Europe a few weeks before his death

◀ 1904 Mahler walk on foot after leaving the Staats Opera of Vienna, Kärntner Strasse, passing through the gate in Augustiner Straße (today Philharmonikerstraße).

his life. Meanwhile, Alma in great secrecy and with some trouble, is divided between the two men that are part of her life. Cruelly she informs her lover of the changes in her husband. She tells him of his reborn love making enthusiasm: *I make him the gift of my life if I stay next to him, I will bring about the death of Gustav if I leave him and he is like a spoiled sick child sick!*

THE MUSIC

"The fair queen is beautiful and will marry only someone who will bring her a red flower, beautiful such as she..."
        Das Klagende Lied

Das Klagende Lied and other lied

Mahler's debut in music is in part a fairy tale, both dramatic and tragic and in tune with the intimate feeling of its author. Mahler was eighteen years old.
Let's talk about the *Das Klagende Lied*. The great passionate Mahlerian lied, which will share with his symphonies and eventually unite in a great work the *Das Liede von de Erde!*
In truth, the composer had already composed three lieder by 1880 in honour of one of his first loves, Josephine Poisl entitled: *Im Lenz, Winterlied e Maitanz im Grünen*. These acted as a forerunner to his first serious work the *Klagende Lied,* the name translated means a song of lamentation and accusation. The composer although young does well, the imprint of genius is already present. Entering the conservatory only three years earlier in Vienna in 1875, Mahler became friends with the contemporary Hugo Wolf (another great liederista) and the older Hans Rott, two tragic figures (both perished in a mental hospital), yet they were important figures in the professional growth of Mahler. The three belonged to the minority party of the Viennese school that did work similar to that of Bruckner and Wagner as opposed to the fashion of the time dictated to by Brahms.
Das Lied Klagende was composed between 1878 and 1880 and already contained the full ingredients of Mahler's style, which was in contrast to the work of Wagner, Schubert and Bruckner. The first draft of this work was more extensive than that which was eventually produced and presented to the public by the author himself who became a famous conductor. The work in fact underwent two revisions, one in 1893 and one in 1898, revisions which involved cutting the entire first part, the *Waldmarchen* (march in the woods). Only in the most recent executions does it return to the insert, Mahler sacrificed this in order to obtain a work which is more balanced. As mentioned, the *Klagende Lied* was presented thanks to his early fame achieved in conducting. In fact Mahler's fame was mainly linked to his ability to director rather than his ability to compose. In this field, his career progressed facilitated by his great talent in this field. Even at 20 years old he was operating in Ljubljana and Olomouc and in 1882 he was deputy director in Kassel.
At 26 years he was in Leipzig and at the age of 28 become Rector of Budapest until he finally became the undisputed 'king' of the Vienna *Staatsoper*. During the years at Kassel he wrote a second set of lieder entitled *Lieder und Gesänge aus der Jugenszeit* (song sung by the youth). These were composed at the end of the draft, and finished in 1891 totalling 14 whilst the first block in 1883 is only made up of five lieds.
In 1884, he completed a fourth round of Lied for example the fourth *Lieder Eines fahrenden Gesellen* (the

HANS ROTT 1858-1884

Rott was born in Vienna, from the relationship between the eighteen year old Maria Rosalia Lutz and the fifty year old Carl Mathias Rott (1807-1876). Both parents were practicing artistic activities. In particular, his father was a quite famous comic actor in Vienna at the time, while his mother was also an actress and a singer. The young Rott was orphaned quite early in 1876, when both his father and his mother died. In the years 1874-1875 he enrolled and attended the *Universität für Musik und darstellende Kunst Wien* (University for music and the executive activities of Vienna), where among others he studied organ with Anton Bruckner. He was considered the best of his students and believed that Rott, not Mahler, would make the future of music. After the death of his parents, there was a change in his fortune and he had to find employment in order to survive. Despite these difficulties he was able to pursue his studies, obtained two awards of honour from the Conservatory, and above all a place as the organist at the church Piaristen (Maria Treu), also getting accommodation at the adjacent monastery. It was in these monastic cells that Rott met his circle of friends, among them Gustav Mahler and Hugo Wolf. He wrote a number of compositions considering the brevity of his life, among them one remembers the Symphony in E flat major for String Orchestra (1874-1875), which was followed by a Final Symphonic two Overture (one from Hamlet and one from Julius Caesar) and a Suite for Orchestra, as well as some lieder, and all the famous Symphony in E major. In 1880, the incident with Johannes Brahms happened. Johannes together with Eduard Hanslick and Karl Goldmark, had to decide who got the assignment of a state scholarship. The great Hamburg composer went so far as to doubt that the symphony in question was actually the work of a young Rott, as claimed: *the songs are associated to many beautiful things, there are so many banal or meaningful things in this composition that they can certainly not be the work of Rott.* Rott, was disappointed, it was a blow that even etched on his mental state. In short he began to give signs of mental disturbance. On 23 October 1880, during a journey, a passenger who was about to light a cigar saw Rott threaten by pulling out a pistol: Because Brahms had filled the train with dynamite, he suddenly extinguished his cigar but Rott threatened to blow up the train. The passengers understood the drama and helped him to calm down. On the same day he was admitted to the General Hospital psychiatric clinic in Vienna, in a state of total confusion.

In the mental hospital he used his manuscripts as toilet paper, shouted and was frantic: *this is the fate that the operas of men deserve.* If he had been looked after better, he could have survived in a decent way, perhaps to be cured or at least improve. His fate, however, was now marked, and from 1881 he attempted suicide for the first time. He was interned at the asylum of the Land of Lower Austria, where he died on 25 June 1884 of tuberculosis. He was not yet 26 years old. At the funeral of the unfortunate musician, Bruckner wanted to attack Brahms, shout that he was responsible for the disaster. He had committed an injustice. But he was too shocked and could not.

wayfarer's songs). It is a cycle composed for the voice and piano. They were written between late 1884 and 1885 New Year's Eve, but only published in 1897. As with previous works, these songs were conceived as a result of a painful private matter, the unhappy love for the singer Johanna Richter, prima donna of the Opera Kassel, the theatre from which Mahler served from 1883 to 1885.

The text was written by Mahler. It was also the last lied after the Poisl to have a text written by the composer, from this point on the texts would be chosen by the professionals of the proses. The best known of the four lied is *Ging heut' morgen übers Feld* (this morning I went to the meadows). The song moves into the parallel key of D major and assumes a trend *In gemächlicher Bewegung* (more placid movement). An initial optimism permeates the song, a modulation is increased which leads the protagonist to the idea of a lost happiness. The theme will be used for the opening of the Symphony no. 1. Interestingly also is the first of the lied with the curious title: *Wenn mein Schatz Hochzeit macht,* (when my love will make her marriage).

When my darling has her wedding-day

When my darling has her wedding,
Joyous wedding,
I will have my day of mourning!
I walk into my closet,
Dark little room,
Weep, weep for my darling,
For my dear darling!
Blümlein blue! not wither!
Sweet little bird You sing on the green heath.
Oh, how is so beautiful the world!
Ziküth! Ziküth!
Do not sing! do not bloom!
Spring is over!
All singing must now.
At night when I go to sleep '
Thought I 'of my sorrow.
Of my sorrow!

As mentioned these are the texts by Mahler, but it must be remembered that a few years after Mahler threw himself into work and completed a theatrical opera play of *Von Weber: Die drei Pintos*.
He was able on that occasion to stumble upon a book in the library belonging to the heirs of Von Weber entitled *Des Knaben Wunderhorn* (The Magically Horn of the Child). This was an anthology of folk songs collected and processed by Achim von Arnim and Clemens Brentano, published in 1805 - 1808. Mahler took from this source the majority of the lyrics for his future Lieder, but he would have had to know at least some of the texts of Arnim - Brentano, as in the first of the series of Lieder published there appeared reworked traces of some verses of the *Eines fahrenden Gesellen*.
In fact it brought about a fundamental reworking of two separate verses of the *Wunderhorn*, which reads: *Denk ich an mein Leide!* (I think of my endless pain!).

The Titan Symphony no. 1 in D major (1887)

Ideal connection to the Lied *eines fahrenden Gesellen*, the first symphony begins with pastoral music by *Ging heut' morgen übers feld* (This morning I went to the fields) where the text reads:

Went over the field this morning,
Dew still hung on the grasses;
Spoke to me the merry finch:
"Why you! Gelt? Good morning! Gelt egg?
You! Will's not a beautiful world?
Zinc! Zinc! Fair and sharp!
How I love the world! "
The bells Blum 'on field
Has me funny, good thing ',
With the bells, sword, sounding,
Your morning greeting rung:
"Will's not a beautiful world?
Ding, ding! Nice thing!
How I love the world! Heia! "
And there began in sunshine
the world suddenly began to glitter;
won all sound and color
In the sunshine!

Flower and bird, great and small!
"Good day, is it not a fine world?
Egg you, eh? Beautiful world?"
Now my happiness also begin?
No, no, I mean,
I can never bloom!

Symphony no. 1 in D major by Gustav Mahler, was composed following a long gestation period between 1887 and 1894. Mahler in those years was more and more involved in the management of his career and did not have much time to devote to the composition. For a long time its author remained undecided whether to consider this work as a symphonic poem or a symphony. In the end it is as known in writing as the first Mahler symphony. This first symphonic work, along with *Klagende* lied and *fahrenden Gesellen Eines* is the first Austrian artist's masterpiece. In the original score, Mahler said: *wie ein naturlaut* (as a sound from nature), a theme that will return in the third symphony. His friend Bauer - Lechner in his memoirs recalled other notes assigned to all the harmonics called to the opera. *To reach the sparkle and shine of the air that I always had in mind.* At the end of the first movement there is a burst of a brass band (perhaps a legacy of the military years at Jglau which were always present in Mahler's mind). It is perhaps the first cut, traditionally then repeated in many of his other compositions. A kind of inner necessity and anxious to break the continuous/regular expression with new ones. The name given to this symphony / symphonic poem is Titan, title borrowed from a novel by Jean Paul, one of Mahler's most beloved writers. However, this title will in the subsequent years be suppressed by the author: *this time I decided to do without the title and the program, not only because I consider them quite inadequate, but more they are not even appropriate...*

The work is planned in four phases with a total duration of about seventy minutes:

I. Langsam , slow schleppend, followed by the allegretto of *Blumine*
II. Kräftig bewegt, doch nicht zu schnell. Joke: Vigorously moved, but not too early
III. Feierlich und gemessen, ohne zu schleppen, Funeral March: Solemn and measured, without dragging
IV. Stürmisch bewegt. Stormily agitated.

▲Gustav Mahler and Richard Strauss awaiting before the opera Salome in Graz in 1906. Note the large difference in height between the two musicians.

"When a true genius appears in this world, you can recognize him by the fact that the idiots all gang up on him."
Jonathan Swift

Rott and Mahler

That which music lost with him was immeasurable: his genius was so high even in his first symphony, which he wrote when he was a young twenty year old and that makes him ñ the word is not strong at all ñ the founder of the new symphony - Gustav Mahler, in his Memoirs of Nathalie Bauer - Lechner

The relations of mutual esteem that bound Rott and Mahler are known. Rott, at the time of his hospitalization at the psychiatric hospital, when he was asked if he remembered who Mahler was, he replied: *Certainly, certainly, Mahler is a genius!*

The symphony no. 1 Mahler or the symphony no. 0 of Rott?

At the time of the rediscovery of the Symphony no. in E major by Rott, part of the international musicology threw itself into focusing on similar tracks between Mahler's first symphony and the work of his old classmate, a risky and possibly misleading operation, which undoubtedly could have led to a rewriting of history of the symphony in the second half of the nineteenth century.
The reaction to elevate Rott to the role of the father of the new symphony was revolutionary as is partially acknowledged by Mahler who was blamed for siphoning compositions of his lesser-known composer friend (his promise to let the public know, as a conductor, the symphony of the unfortunate friend was not in fact ever maintained).
In fact, more attentive and less superficial analysis performed on both works, give unmistakable signs of the presence of each other's musical influences. And if the matter goes to influence, then it is also fair to say, that according to some critics that link will be maintained at least until Mahler's Fifth Symphony. In this regard, the musicologist Wolfgang Fuhrmann had this to say: *The symphony number Zero of Rott or the first of Mahler? And to add: Inevitably Rott and Mahler must have had an intimate interchange of musical ideas.*
The symphony of Rott, set in E major has truly original sounds, but the feature that now makes it known to the ears of contemporary listeners more than a century later appears to be the distinctly Mahlerian.
Mahler always bestowed high esteem and the presence of genius towards his friend. Rott was unable to enter the hall of famous musicians because he died too early and he did not have the means and tools to develop his complete talent.
Mahler, is instead one that has done it, reaching the summit even for his friend.
Neophytes and partisans of Rott claim without exaggeration that Mahler plundered more than a few ideas of Rott, thematic ideas, rhythm, timbre, then reworked and served diligently in his symphonies, at least until the symphony number five. But being a genius he was also to improve them.
In addition to the joke of his First Symphony, tracks and atmosphere also found in the second and the next three.
With time and with the disappearance of Rott, Mahler makes an increasingly diaphanous ghost with less presence. Of course if they met in their forties in 1900, perhaps Mahler would be disappointed by Rott and Rott would have asked: *what have you become Gustav?*

▲ Gustav Mahler at the direction of Italian orchestra during his visit to Rome.

"Auferstehung" Resurrection Symphony no. 2 in C minor

I called the first Totenfeier and, if you ask me, this is the hero of my First Symphony which I bring to bury.
Gustav Mahler

The first of the four great Mahlerian symphonies in which the item appears, and one of my favourites, the *Resurrection* had a very long gestation period. The first movement was introduced immediately after the close of the first symphony in 1888, while the closure was completed six years later in December 1894. Those were the years of hard work as a conductor and Mahler did not have much time to compose.
After Budapest in 1891 he was called to direct the Hamburg theatre, and was then considered one of the world's music authorities.
The text of the Second Symphony are among the first to arrive by the often cited *Das Knaben Wunderhorn*, the collection of German medieval songs found in the house Von Weber. One of these lieds, *Des Antonius von Padua Fischpredigt* (the preaching to the fish by Saint Antonio from Padova), was almost literally transcribed like a joke, while the Lied *Urlicht* (light primitive) became the 4th movement.
In Hamburg, Mahler also met the famous conductor Hans von Bülow. He had a very high regard for him and was a major supporter of Mahler's artistic directive talent, however, he did not consider particularly interesting to say the least his compositional work. At a presentation of these works, Bulow showed irritation in having to hear them. This fact contributed in the delay in the completion of that work, which then sped up again due to von Bulow. He passed away in 1894, and Mahler was able to listen to the ode function Lutheran entitled *Aufersthen!* (Will rise).
It was the missing link, the word order. It was for Mahler, as claimed by the key psychoanalytic student of Freud, Theodor Reik a kind of liberation by the rejection of Bulow. A kind of symbiosis between the admiration of his directive talent and the reserve for the composer's works.

Urlicht (Primeval Light)

O little red rose!
Man lies in greatest need!
Man lies in greatest pain!
Even more would I rather be in heaven!
There I came upon a broad path.
There came an angel and wanted to turn me away.
Ah no, I would not be turned away!
Ah no, I would not be turned away:
I am from God and want to return to God!
The loving God will give me a little of the light,
will illuminate me into the eternal blessed life!

Mahler wanted to call the first movement *Totenfeier* (celebration of the death) symbolically dedicating it to the hero of his first symphony Titan: *Titan who took to the grave, and whose life I observe in a clear mirror, as seen watching from above. And then suddenly emerges the question: Why did you live?*
The central part of the symphony is understood as an interlude until the explosion at the end that repeats the existential questions mentioned in the first movement.
After the agony of the first movement and the round about of the joke, the human being returns to the age of childhood, finally freed from uncertainty and doubt: *a first ray of light shines in the next movement.*
The famous fourth movement *Urlicht* in D flat major, follows almost without interruption the preceding movement, the text is based on the Lied of the same name taken from the collection *Des Knaben Wunderhorn*. It is the prelude to the grand finale. It has a solemn and ethereal character: Mahler wanted the rival to sing it like a child who imagines he has arrived in paradise. And in fact it is this impression that has attracted me to this work.
Perhaps only *Beato Angelico* (in painting) was able to give as good an idea of what it means to feel, see, or go to heaven as Mahler has succeeded (in music) with his second symphony. The human voice, used here for the first time, is in the foreground, backed by a kind of delicate fanfare of brass instruments. Themes that refer to another great symphony for chorus, voice and orchestra by Mahler, the number 8.
The last monumental movement, very long (over 37 minutes) is an instrumental mystical intensity, which reached its peak in the angelic intervention by a soprano and anticipated by flutes which in turn anticipate the chorus that is leading the way with the arrival of the voice of the singer who reaches and exceeds the vocal range of the chorus, reminding us of paradise for a second and final time. Great !!
Today, at least the program of the symphony seems dated, son of a fatalistic idea so fashionable in Europe during the late nineteenth century, in my opinion, however it is strongly redeemed and an incomparable pathos that manages to offer to the listener.
We can point out among the many performances of this great symphony one directed by Claudio Abbado at the Lucerne festival with Eteri Gvazava soprano and mezzo-soprano Anna Larsson.
In its final form, the symphony is divided into five movements:

1st Mit durchaus ernstem feierlichem und Ausdruck (Allegro maestoso. With absolutely serious and solemn expression)
2nd Sehr gemächlich (Andante moderate. Very comfortable)
3rd In ruhig flie fl ender Bewegung (with quiet and smooth movement)
4th Urlichtî (primitive Light) - *Sehr feierlich, aber Schlicht* (very solemn but simply, as a choral)
5th Wild herausfahrend. Auferstehíní (time to joke. Wild, vigorous, slow and mysterious)

The last one contains the hymn *idie Auferstehungî* (The Resurrection) by Friedrich Klopstock.

Symphony no. 3 in D minor, the feast of nature

Symphony no. 3 in D minor by Gustav Mahler, was composed between the summers of 1893 and 1896, and performed for the first time in 1902. This is the longest symphony ever written, it lasts on average 95 minutes. It belongs to the monumental symphonies, alongside the second and eighth.

The lyrical testimony of the entire operation is his friend Natalie Bauer - Lechner, for who Mahler leaves all his impressions not without a certain enthusiasm. In fact, this is certainly one of his most unorganised symphonies.

Everything here has been encoded in terms of strict step by steps, prepared with his legendary patience and uncompromising perfection. Very inspired, and this is why it took him two summers at Steinbach to finish, despite its enormous size, although it must be said that the first sketches date back to four years previously.

This symphony also represented a clear break with respect to the first two symphonies, a bit fatalistic in relation to the ideal program. In it there appears for the first time the rich palette of colors and scenes that accompany Mahler throughout the rest of his musical production.

The third symphony belongs to the Wunderhorn - symphonies. The text of the vocals comes in fact from this unique gospel that Mahler used for all his first works and lieds.

The third symphony continues the path taken by Mahler in his second symphony, the rest or gestation is taken together and is often twisted. However, this is were the similarities end and these do not continue into the soul and essence of the two symphonies.

The symphony is defined by multiple parts of nature and it is in this light that Mahler prepared it. Themes that bind the relationship between man and nature. The nickname which is the most widely used for this is the singing of the great Pan, with obvious references to *Nietzchiani*, also for the presence of text derived from the work of the German thinker. As stated by Zarathustra: *My symphony will be something the world has not yet heard. Nature speaks in here and tells secrets so deep that perhaps we can only sense this in dreams. Sometimes I feel really uncomfortable and it does not seem like I composed it: just because I can achieve what I want.*

In short, an inspired Mahler is satisfied with his work so as to define it as birth in a sort of dream state.

The symphony is divided into six movements:

1st Pan erwacht. Der Sommer ein marschiert (Pan awakes, the summer comes) *Kr‰ftig entschieden* (Strong and resolute) This first movement is long and lasts for about 35 minutes.
2nd Was mir die Blumen auf der Wiese erzählen (that which the flowers of the meadow tell me) Tempo di Menuetto
3rd Was mir die Tiere im Walde erzählen (what the animals of the forest tell me) Comodo (joking)
4th Was mir der Mensch erzählt (what man tells me) *Sehr langsam* - Mysterious (Very slow - mysterious)
5th Was mir die Engel erzählen (what the angels tell me) *Lustig im* Tempo *und keck im Ausdruck* (in a vibrant and bold in expression)
6th Was mir die Liebe erzählen (what love tells me) *Langsam - Ruhevoll - Empfunden* (slowly, in a quiet, deeply felt mood)

Symphony no. 4 in G major, a normal symphony

Symphony no. 4 of Gustav Mahler was composed between the summers of 1899 and 1900. Unlike the previous long and majestic symphony, the fourth is one of the most contained and reduced symphonies.

There is singing in this symphony, but in this case only in the final intervention of the soprano with no other voices, choirs etc.

The fourth is also the first Viennese symphony. In fact, as early as April 1897 Mahler was appointed rector of the court in the Habsburg capital and was staunchly defended by Emperor Franz Joseph, who liked to say: *Touch everything but not my director at Staatsoper...*

In terms of numbers, it is also the last symphony of the Wunderhorn cycle, the lied which constitutes the

▲ 1905, Vienna, Moll's backyard. (19, 10 Wollergasse) - Max Reinhardt, Gustav Mahler, Carl Moll, Hans Pfitzner and presumably Josef Hoffmann.

entire last movement: *Das leben himmlische* is the ideal closure of a literary and musical passion which ends here. The genesis of this symphony, at least initially is directly linked to the original project of the Third symphony. This symphony, in fact, consisted originally of seven movements, the last of which was entitled 'What a boy tells me'. This lied that appears in the fourth was originally meant to end in the third. The fourth, then becomes a sort of reflection on the themes of death and childhood, though done with ironic traits.

Also for this reason it is tied to his childhood, this symphony maintains a character of the score. Here Mahler is content with a traditional orchestra as seen in the earlier symphonies. Thus an organic one without trombones and tuba, nor double horns, a lighter orchestra, which also appears functional to a music that is linked to the Baroque times, played in the form of a sonata, rondo with variation, the final Lied.

The Fourth Symphony then occupies a special place in the symphonic works of Gustav Mahler. Firstly it concludes the cycle of the Wunderhorn - Symphonien, by contrast it inaugurates a new style, a more personal and intimate one which is less prone to monumentality.

As for size, it is contained in four parts, Mahler declared to the omnipresent Natalie Bauer - Lechner: *Actually I just wanted to write a humorous symphony, and what came out was a normal size symphony, whereas before, when I thought of having to compose a symphony, what would emerge was a work which lasted three times as much as was the case of the Second and the Third.*

The organizational chart of the symphony is in four movements for orchestra and soprano solo, as follows:

1st Bedächtig, Nicht eilen, recht gemächlich (Thoughtful, not rushed, very convenient)
2nd Im gemächlicher Bewegung, (With quiet movement, Unhurried)
3rd Ruhevoll (Calm)
4th Sehr behaglich "Das himmlische Leben" (Very conveniently The heavenly life) for solo soprano with text from *Das Knaben Wunderhorn.*

Das himmlische leben *"The Heavenly Life"*
(from Des Knaben Wunderhorn)

We enjoy heavenly pleasures
and therefore avoid earthly ones.
No worldly tumult
is to be heard in heaven.
All live in greatest peace.
We lead angelic lives,
yet have a merry time of it besides.
We dance and we spring,
We skip and we sing.
Saint Peter in heaven looks on.

John lets the lambkin out,
and Herod the Butcher lies in wait for it.
We lead a patient,
an innocent, patient,

▲ 1905, Vienna, Moll's backyard. Another picture as the previous one which portrays the typical lively cultural center of the *Felix Austria* in the early twentieth century.

▶ An autograph letter of Gustav Mahler, the typical writing a little neurotic ...

Musik wird immer zudringlicher ab-
gefordert wird, kann dies nicht sein.
Ich hoffe, Sie ins fühle aus Ihren Worten,
dass gerade Sie dies begreifen, und
Jeder aus dem Wesen meiner Musik
heraus, welche aus sich allein, und
ihren inneren — weder in Bildern noch
durch "Inhaltsangaben"   — wohl festzubarten —
Bedingungen erfasst werden will.
Mögen Sie mir, lieber Herr Schuster,
ein solcher werden! Ich weiß nicht,
ob Sie schon (früher) in der Lage waren, von
meinem Schaffen Notiz zu nehmen.
Es liegen ein e Reihe meiner Parti-
turen vor, die ich Ihnen, wenn Sie es
wünschen, gerne zu Senden werde.
Für heute nur wahrend den tief-
gefühlten Dank meines ganz
Unverstandenen. (Ja noch ärger:
Mißverstandenen)
Ihr sehr ergebener
Gustav Mahler

dear little lamb to its death.
Saint Luke slaughters the ox
without any thought or concern.
Wine doesn't cost a penny
in the heavenly cellars;
The angels bake the bread.

Good greens of every sort
grow in the heavenly vegetable patch,
good asparagus, string beans,
and whatever we want.
Whole dishfuls are set for us!
Good apples, good pears and good grapes,
and gardeners who allow everything!
If you want roebuck or hare,
on the public streets
they come running right up.

Should a fast day come along,
all the fishes at once come swimming with joy.
There goes Saint Peter running
with his net and his bait
to the heavenly pond.
Saint Martha must be the cook.

There is just no music on earth
that can compare to ours.
Even the eleven thousand virgins
venture to dance,
and Saint Ursula herself has to laugh.
There is just no music on earth
that can compare to ours.
Cecilia and all her relations
make excellent court musicians.
The angelic voices
gladden our senses,
so that all awaken for joy.

▲▼ Two images of Mahler child. above in 1889 with his brother Otto who then eventually committed suicide at twenty-one years. Below Gustav at the age of about 8/9 years.

▶ Caricature of Mahler. The translated caption says: *why would we have to pay these big salaries?*

Five Lieder on the text of Friedrich Ruckert Lieder for voice and orchestra, 1901-1902

In my humble opinion, these lieder are absolute masterpieces. These along with *Das Lied von der Erde* represent a collection of amazing lieds, dense, full-bodied, very cultured and refined. On all accounts, *Ich bin der Welt Ahbanden gekommen* lied in a certain sense is a tribute to the fifth symphony written in that time. Mahler used for these the text by Ruckert.

1st Blicke mir nicht in die Lieder (Look away from my songs) *Sehr lebhaft* very lively (F major)
2nd Ich einen linden Duft atmeti (I breath a gentle fragrance) *Sehr zart und innig* very delicate and intimate (D major)
3rd Ich bin der Welt abhanden gekommen (are now lost to the world) *fuflerst langsam und zur‚ckhaltend* extremely slow and cautious (F major)
4th Um mitternacht (at midnight) *Ruhig, gleichmäßig* Quiet and uniform in style.
5th Liebst du um Schoenheit (loved for the beauty) *Innig* sincere

Liebst du um Schoenheit (If you love for beauty)

If you love for beauty, O love not me!
Love the sun, She has golden hair!
If you love for youth, O love not me!
Love the spring, The young every year!
You love for treasure, O do not love me.
Love the mermaid, that has a lot of beads clear.
If you love for love, Oh, love me!
Love me ever, Love you 'I evermore.

Who was Fiderick Ruckert

Friedrich Ruckert (1788 - 1866) was a late-romantic poet, translator, scholar and professor of German oriental languages. His influence was mainly in the musical realm.

Many of the greatest German composers were fascinated by Ruckert choosing to turn his verses into music: Schubert, Robert and Clara Schumann, Brahms, Loewe, Mahler (*Kindertotenlieder* and 5 Ruckert - Lieder for voice and orchestra), Richard Strauss, Zemlinsky, Hindemith, Bartuk, Berg, Hugo Wolf and Heinrich Kaspar Schmid. For a total of about 121 poems he was only surpassed by Goethe, Heine and Rilke.

The collection of the Five Lieder on poems by Ruckert were composed between 1901 and 1904, and published in 1905, i.e. in the same period of Mahler's Fifth and Sixth Symphony and *Kindertotenlieder* on texts by Ruckert. The first, third and fourth were written in the summer of 1901, simultaneously with the first three *Kindertotenlieder*, the second was composed in 1903 for his wife and finally the fifth in 1904. In these Lieder Mahler breathed a melancholy twilight and meaning of life, according to a vision particularly fashionable in the early twentieth century.

In using these versions of the collection, he did not follow precise scales since Mahler did not leave any precise indication on the execution order of the five Lieder on texts Ruckert, unlike what occurred with *Kindertotenlieder*.

It depends essentially on the choice of the singer which can be a soprano or a baritone. Personally I like more the soprano version, and specifically suggest the execution of the mezzo-soprano Magdalena Kožená conducted by Claudio Abbado

▼ Netherlands 1909 Gustav Mahler encircled by Dutch colleagues in the offices of the Royal Concertgebouw, Amsterdam.

Symphony no. 5 in C minor

I breathed in a sweet scent! There was a linen branch in the room. Gift of a loved hand.

The symphony no. 5 in C minor in five movements by Gustav Mahler was written between 1901 and 1902 in Maiernigg in Carinthia, in the famous villa on the lake, in fact in the cabin nestled in the woods. The first two movements constitute Part I, the long central joke Part II, whilst Part III belongs to the last two movements. Perhaps the most famous symphony of Mahler and certainly one of the most listened to. Some passages like the noted Adagietto represent the culmination of Mahler's music. Among the symphonies of Mahler this is my favourite one along with the second, the first movement of the Ninth and the andante of the sixth. After this personal interlude, we return to the analysis of the work.

The symphony was also made famous by the film director Luchino Visconti, who inserted it in an appropriate way in his masterpiece Death in Venice, where in addition to the music, even the protagonist was a striking reminder of the Austrian musician. Defined in C minor but made up of various tones, specified by Mahler given the difference of each individual movement. The first is in fact in C sharp minor, the second in A minor, the third in D major, the fourth in F major and the fifth in D major.

The Fifth symphony, original and sophisticated is configured as said on several occasions in the same way in which Mahler recounted tragic events via the orchestra. And as with the First symphony where Titan who fights and dies, so with the Fifth he invents an extraordinary journey into the wilderness. As on other occasions the festival will open with a sad funeral march that is presented more as a prologue than as a 1st movement, a role that is assigned instead to the second is a kind of Allegro in sonata form.

Adorno's observation of this movement is that it resembles the shape of the novel, in the sense that it introduces new themes, elaborates themes already used but redresses this to appear unusual.

The second part is constituted by the other three movements. Joke on the third and Rondo in the sparkling fourth which is very enjoyable to listen to, and in the middle of the absolute masterpiece is the Adagietto, which became in time a great representative signature for the composer. The third movement, the Joke in D major is the highest exaltation of polyphony and is marked by movements in the form of the Viennese waltz, which perfectly interpenetrates one another. In the fourth the Adagietto is as mentioned above the most famous of Mahler's pieces.

We are faced with a mystical lyrical oasis, extremely delicate and inspired song, very moving, entrusted only to strings and harp. Thematically it draws on previous work like the Lied *Ich bin der Welt abhanden gekommenî* (I am lost to the world), the third of Ruckert - Lieder. This beautiful fourth movement takes the listener on a dimension almost dreamlike ethereal, diaphanous and magical.

"Ich bin der Welt abhanden gekommen" ("I am lost to the world")

I am lost to the world
with which I used to waste so much time,
It has heard nothing from me for so long
that it may very well believe that I am dead!
It is of no consequence to me
Whether it thinks me dead;
I cannot deny it,
for I really am dead to the world.
I am dead to the world's tumult,
And I rest in a quiet realm!
I live alone in my heaven,
In my love and in my song!

Finally the fifth movement (Rondo - Finale. Allegro in D major) takes the energy of the third after the suspension of paradise of the movement which preceded it.

1st Trauermarsch: In gemessenem Schritt. Streng. Wie ein Kondukt. (Funeral March. A measured pace, stern, like a funeral procession).

2nd Stürmisch bewegt, mit größter Vehemenz (stormily moving with great vehemence)

3rd Scherzo. Kräftig, nicht zu schnell. (Joke. Vigorous, not too fast)

4th Adagietto. Sehr langsam (Adagietto. Very slow)

5th Rondo - Finale. Allegro (Rondo - Finale. Lively and joyous)

Kindertotenlieder (Songs for the dead children) for voice and orchestra on texts by Friedrich Ruckert

1st Nun will die Sonn' so hell aufgehin - (Today the sun wants to rise and shine again) *Langsam und schwerm, tig; nicht schleppend* (D minor) Slow in an unrestrained way

2nd Nun sehí ich wohl, warum so dunkle Flammen (Now I see why flames are so dark) - *Ruhig, nicht schleppend* (C minor) Quiet and not repressed

3rd Wenn dein Mutterlein - (When your goodness) *Schwer, dumpf* (C minor) Heavy and boring

4th Oft Denki ich, sie sind nur ausgegangen - (I often think they are just out for a walk) *Ruhig bewegt, ohne zu Eilen* (E flat minor) calm and without haste.

5th In diesem Wetter - (In this weather, in this storm) *Mit ruhelos schmerzvollem Ausdruck* (D minor) with full expression restless pain.

In 1901 there occurred several important things in the life of Mahler. Starting with a period of severe illness in February due to haemorrhage and convalescence in March during his Fourth Symphony.
In November, their appeared on the scene the young Alma Schindler, who became his wife in March 1902.
In the field of music there is a growing new Fifth Symphony, this time disconnected from lied. The texts of Arnim and Brentano's *Des Knaben Wunderhorn* are retired, faithful companions of Mahler in the first part of his composition career.
And in this context the idea of the five *Kindertotenlieder* (on R‚ckert texts) matures.
They were written between June 1901 (the first three) and the 1904 summer (the last two). Mahler wrote them six years before the tragic death of his daughter Maria at the age of four. Alma will always interpreted these as a curse and will never forgive her husband.
Abandoned the world in the Wunderhorn, Mahler intends to distance himself from the comforting world of the folktale, as was suggested in the verses of the *Lied Ich bin der Welt abhanden gekommenî*, his musical self-portrait written in August 1901.
In these lied pessimism and fatalism reach cosmic heights, and do not leave any room for joy and redemption. Even to the apparent innocence of childhood life, he lived this as an illusion of happiness with absolute emptiness. The five Lieder exist in a surreal light and leaves one feeling empty. In this collection, somebody wanted to see the aesthetic combination with the fashion of the time - a kind of funeral *Jugendstil* in the succession of images which are unreal and this became the supporting line.

▶ The misfortunes in the house Mahler did not affect children only, as in the case of most of Mahler brothers or the death is his daughter, in some ways reminded the Kindertotenlieder.
as Jews suffered a sad fate during the terrible years of Nazism.
The most famous victim was the granddaughter Alma Rosé (1906 -1944) by Justine daughter and granddaughter of Gustav Mahler. Talented violinist was deported by the Nazis in the concentration camp of Auschwitz-Birkenau. Here for ten long months, he directed an orchestra of detainees, under the terrible blackmail of being suppressed in every moment. Rosé fact died in the concentration camp due to a sudden illness, caused by a food poisoning.

Oft denk' ich, sie sind nur ausgegangen (I often think: they have only just gone out)

and now they will be coming back home.
The day is fine, don't be dismayed,
They have just gone for a long walk.
Yes indeed, they have just gone out,
and now they are making their way home.
Don't be dismayed, the day is fine,
they have simply made a journey to yonder heights.

They have just gone out ahead of us,
and will not be thinking of coming home.
We go to meet them on yonder heights
In the sunlight, the day is fine
On yonder heights.

Symphony no. 6 in A minor, the Tragic

Symphony no. 6 Gustav Mahler composed in the summers between 1903 and 1904 and finished the instrumentation in 1905. The first performance took place in Essen, Germany on 27 May 1906, conducted by the composer himself. Revised and published in 1906. The symphony lasted about 80 minutes and is commonly known as Tragic (title which is not yet clear whether attributed to Mahler).

The meaning of the title is in recognition of the negative character of the symphony. Dedicated to his wife and it also contains a specific theme of Alma, as Mahler himself said that he tried to sum up Alma's character and personality.

The four tempos present a united tone entirely unusual for Mahler: three out of four movements in fact are in the home key. It is also the only symphony of Mahler to end with a minor key movement (all the other symphonies, even the most dramatic, have a positive final like the First or Fifth, or at least serene as the Wunderhorn symphonies - or Ninth).

The sixth also belongs to these symphonies with the hammer, just due to the inclusion of those hammer blows, crashing down like deadly blows of fate to score the hero's end. Inserts perhaps serving the author due to the difficult search for a formal balance in the presence of a symphony marked by incomplete elucidated music full of rhetorical redundancy.

The composer himself said: *My Sixth is a puzzling solution of which can only be attempted by a generation that has embraced and assimilated my first five symphonies.*

The symphony is divided, as already said, in four movements, however, the order as they appear today has been the subject of some debate.

On the occasion of the first performance, the Joke was in second position (the current), before the Andantes. Mahler later changed his mind and reversed the two movements.

However, in 1907, a change in the program and Mahler re-established the early indications, it is still the most frequently proposed by conductors of orchestras.

One of the best-known pupils and neophytes of Mahler, Alban Berg said about the symphony the only sixth despite Beethoven's Pastoral.

This is the final list:

1st Heftig, aber markig energetic Joyous and energetic

2nd Wuchtig, Heavy joke

3rd Andante moderate 4/4

4th Finale (Moderate joy, cut off time)

My favourite remains the third movement, a moderate Andante in E flat major run with very subtle nuances and still favours the arches, the orchestration seems to flow by an introduction of a phrasing in ten bars which recalls the pathos of an elegy almost whispered.

The second theme is exposed by the English horn which gives the melody a nearly pastoral trend, but with rougher accents and less twilight. The incredible effectiveness are then the two harps, which can interrupt the dramatic atmosphere that reverberates from the first half and outpourings in a delicate chisel of work that at times seems to evoke the poignant Adagietto of the Fifth Symphony.

▲ Another customary caricature dedicated to Mahler, often the target of critics and satirists of the time. This is dedicated to the sixth symphony.
The translated caption says: *My God I forgot the horn! Now I can not write a symphony ...*

Symphony no. 7 in A minor, the Tragic

Symphony no. 7 in A minor by Gustav Mahler was written between 1904 and 1906, and is in five movements. One of the curious features of this symphony is the unprecedented use of some curious instruments such as the guitar, mandolin, baritone horn and cowbell.

The first performance of the Seventh took place on 19 September 1908 in Prague, on the occasion of the celebrations of the Jubilee of Emperor Franz Joseph.

The Seventh is among the nine of the most difficult and complex symphonies of Mahler, according to the composer himself, who worked in a fit of rage - as he told his wife Alma - during the summer of 1905 in an atmosphere of almost total isolation. The seventh has its great admirers, and for many of them this symphony is the best. Some analysts think that this is the origin of the twelve-tone technique, although to me this seems like a risky view given the bulk melody contained in it.

Since his first Symphony this had mediocre success, but aroused considerable interest in the music. The seventh and the eight are the least performed in repertory.

Especially Schnberg and Berg expressed favourable opinions on this powerful composition (its duration is around more than 90 minutes) with reference particularly to certain harmonic inventions and certain orchestral mixes expressing extraordinary values.

The orchestra of Mahler's Seventh is rich in ideas, also new and using well-researched colors to emphasize the psychological and descriptive situations taking place in Mahler's inner mind which he expressed in his music, which were far away from any illustrative intention. Definitely an intimate and intellectual work, a kind of alter ego with a humoresque character and light (using the fourth as an example).

The five timings of the symphony

1st Langsam (Adagio). *Nicht schleppen* - resolute Allegro, but not too much

2nd Nachtmusik (Night Music). Allegro moderate

3rd Joke. Schattenhaft - Trio

4th Nachtmusik. Andante amoroso

5th Rondo - Finale. Tempo I (ordinary Allegro) - Tempo II (Allegro moderate but energetic)

Authoritative sources inform one that Mahler used jokes on the final Rondo, one which has the most curious timing and proceed together throughout the symphony, like a contradiction, a subterfuge where Mahler even gets to mention Wagner's Maestri *cantori di Nürnberg*.

The musician indicated the bold character of his rondo with a typically Austrian saying: *I was Kosti die Welt, How much does the world cost me!*

The world represented that which oppressed him daily, the fierce struggles of his fans and detractors of his work in Vienna, with its miseries, meanness, falsity, misunderstandings, which made huge demands on him and how he survived as a composer.

In nature (theme already used in the third) Mahler had identified freedom, purity, and the true creator of life, sent to earth not so much to make up, but to be made up of the voices of nature, there he had fixed the boundaries of spontaneity. The Seventh Symphony is four-fifths a tragedy, poignant and brutal parting from nature and the final rondo is dedicated to the world.

▲ Gustav Mahler with a curious white hat and his friend Bruno Walter in Prague on September 19, 1908. On the occasion of the world premiere of the composer's Seventh Symphony

Symphony no. 8 in E flat major called the Thousand

Symphony no. 8 is the most majestic symphony of Mahler, also called the Thousand due to the large number of people needed for its execution both between orchestral and mixed choirs. At the first performance the author directed the 858 elements of the choir and 171 of the orchestra.
The Symphony was composed in Maiernigg between 1906 and 1907. The entire work consists of two parts, and was composed in one moment of inspiration, in the shed located near the composer's villa on Lake Worthersee in Carinthia. It is also the last work composed after the death of his eldest daughter Maria Anna Putzie. After this tragic event, the Mahler family decided to leave the house which was tied to this tremendous grief. From that moment, the new (and last) place of composition of Mahler become Dobbiaco where he was born (always in a wooden shed built in the woods) *Das Liede von der Erde*, the Ninth and Tenth Symphony or rather parts of that tenth as it is actually an unfinished symphony. As in the previous three symphonies also the eighth was dedicated to his wife Alma.
As already said about the Seventh Symphony, the eighth due to its wasteful deployment was very poorly represented. Only in recent years we are witnessing a tremendous revival of this symphony which has witnessed a recovery of many recordings of this symphony which is sung with majestic character as the second and the eighth note.
The structure of the symphony is particularly atypical, it is conventionally divided into 4 or 5 movements, but it is composed of two parts, connected by common themes and the theme of redemption by way of love.

1st Part I in Latin: *Veni, creator spiritus*. This first part is based on an early medieval hymn.

2nd Part II in German: final scene of *Goethe Fausti (Schlußszene aus Goethes "Faust")*.

What did Mahler think of his Eighth Symphony?

I've never written anything like this, in content and style, this new work is something completely different from my other works, and is certainly the biggest thing I've ever done, maybe I've never worked under the impulse of such constriction, and it was like a vision of lightning: suddenly everything was right before my eyes, and it was enough to put it on paper, as if it had been dictated...

This Eighth Symphony presents special characters which combines two poems in two different languages, the first part is a Latin hymn and the second part is nothing less than the final scene of Faust. You wonder? I have long wanted to make this scene of hermits close with glory, and so different from what everyone else did that they set to music so sweet and weak; but right now I had not thought of that.

By chance I recently had the joy of getting hold of an old book, and I opened it at the Veni, creator spiritus hymn, and all of a sudden it stood before me: not only the first theme, but the entire first half, and as a response I could not find anything more beautiful than the words of Goethe in the scene of hermits!

But also in form the Eighth is something completely new: can you imagine a symphony sung from beginning to end? So far I have used the word and always only the human voice to explain, as a synthetic expression factor, to tell with precision that which is only possible with words to be able to express this in purely symphonic expressions using huge amplitude.

But the human voice here is both an instrument; the entire first tempo is set in a strictly symphonic form and yet is completely sung. Yet it is strange that so far nobody has thought of this idea - it is the egg of Columbus: the Symphony itself, where the most beautiful instrument that exists has led to fulfil his destiny - and not just as sound, because the human voice is also the bearer of poetry.

All the symphonies composed by Mahler, without exception, refers to the character or genre of the initial movement, the one that preceded it; in this respect, each has its own personal character. This is even truer for the eighth, in fact this one is just unique.

At the beginning of the Eighth Symphony, there is a sudden explosion produced by a colossal, majestic and varied set of choral and orchestral masses which gives us a unique and sublime experience with the first attack of the organ and then the phrases of the *Veni Creator Spiritus!*

An indirect confirmation of the overwhelming and impetuous of that initial burst of creativity we are given access to Alma's views who describes the events of that summer on the lake: *After our arrival in Maiernigg, there were, like every year, usually two weeks in which he was haunted by the lack of inspiration, then one morning as he crossed the threshold of his studio in the woods, suddenly he remembered the Veni, creator spiritus. He composed in a very short time the entire opening chorus of those remembered fragments of the text. But the words and the music did not fit: the music overwrites the text. In the throes of an excited telegraph to Vienna which he himself sent by telegram the entire text of the ancient Latin psalm.*

The full text coincided perfectly with the music: intuitively he had composed the music for each stanza.

The problem as noted by some critics was, if anything, the relationship that bound the *Veni , creator spiritus* and the Chorus mysticus of Faust, moreover in two different languages, Latin and German (Mahler evidently loved the difficulties and extreme challenges). However they (the two texts) are cues on how to recognize in the rationalist view of Goethe. Ending by reliving a similar philosophical logic.

The first performance of the Eighth Symphony or Symphony of a Thousand was conducted by the composer himself. It took place in the new concert hall in the Exhibition Park of the city 12 September 1910.

It was an unprecedented event and unlike any of the premiere of Mahler. Bruno Walter, who was present, witnessed the great Mahler euphoria as he hurried back to the stage until the chorus of children walking along single file, each clutching small hands outstretched toward him. Of course there was also the dedicatee Alma who said: *Waiting for Monaco and all of those who had come from outside to attend this premiere was huge.*

Already the dress rehearsal had entranced everyone. But the enthusiasms of execution exceeded all bounds. With Mahler's appearance on the podium the entire audience stood up. A perfect silence. It was the most moving tribute that has ever been done to an artist. I was on a stage about to pass out from pure emotions.
In this symphony, which rises to superhuman heights, subdues enormous masses and transforms them into light sources. It was an indescribable experience, how indescribable was the success that followed: *everyone rushed to Mahler. After we spent an evening happy and peaceful during which Mahler was acclaimed and complimented by all ... Finally, we remained conversing till the morning with Gucki (*Anna, the second daughter of Mahler*), our dear child sleeping beside us.*

Mahler described the Eighth Symphony as his most grand or even a gift to the nation. These statements have sometimes been misunderstood as signs of a latent feeling of nationalism or cultural imperialism, which badly scarred our knowledge of his personality and of his socialistic sympathies in politics. The more creative essence is still in the binomial assessment and we in the relationship between creative spirit and Eros. An unprecedented idea in those Freudian years transposed by Mahler in the way he knew how, goes on to say in the sublime music, the fundamental relationship between creativity and sexuality, that sexuality is finally recognized as a source of creativity. The Eighth Symphony with its impetuous pace magnificently proclaims that the Eros is - in the words of the same Mahler - *the real creator of the world.*

▲ Large photo of the group at the execution of the eighth Mahler symphony the next year by the great composer's death in. You can recognize among the others Alexander von Zemlinsky (front row, second from left), Arnold Schoenberg, third from left, and Franz Schreker fourth from left, along with many members of the Vienna Philharmonic Choir.

Symphony no. 9 in D major

In the fall of 1912 Alban Berg wrote to his wife: *I played again Mahler's Ninth. The first movement is the most splendid that Mahler wrote. The expression of an unheard love for this land, the desire (Sehnsucht) to live in peace with nature and to be able to enjoy it to its full, in all its depth, before the coming of death. Because that arrives with no escape.*

The whole movement is permeated by the premonition of death. It presents itself continually. Every dream culminates in this (hence the constantly renewed agitation that grows impetuous after the most delicate steps), to the maximum degree when the premonition of death becomes a certainty, in which death itself announces itself with incredible strength right in the middle of the deepest and most painful joy of living. And then the mournful solo violin and viola and those soldierly sounds: *the death in armour. Against all this there is no more resistance. What comes to me seems like resignation. Always with the thought of the afterlife, which is manifested at that very mysterious step similar to the thin air far above the mountains - yes, like in the space that becomes more rarefied (Ether).* And again, for the last time, Mahler turns to the land, not the struggles and actions, which rids itself (as in the *Lied von der Erde,* with mordant descending chromatic passages), but now completely to nature. *How and how long you still want to enjoy the beauties of the earth!* Far from any trouble, he wants to put the home (*Heimat*) in the free and pure air of *Semmerin,* to take a deep breath of this air, the purest of this land, with more and more deep breaths, because this heart, the most splendid that ever beat amongst men, could spread more and more, before having to stop beating.

Who better than Berg, the spiritual disciple of Mahler could describe this great symphony.

The first half was really great, absolutely one of the best things written by the composer.

The ninth is not only the last fully completed work of the author, (the tenth as we known will only have sketches for the first movement and little else), but also the swan song of the history of the symphony, which with the ninth reaches its peak following 150 years of life.

This final work (with the tenth and *Das Lied von der Erde)* all designed and composed in Dobbiaco, during the last stage in the life of Mahler are also considered sinister due to their name, the death trilogy which coincides with Mahler's health problems following the betrayal of Alma and again a few years before the death of his daughter at Maiernigg. It was the death of the little girl which made Mahler discover Dobbiaco and made him abandon the house in Carinzia. He moved to Alt - Schluderbach in South Tyrol, near Dobbiaco. The different landscape reflects the profound transformation which took place in the soul of the musician. Here he immediately built his wooden hut, not too far from the farm where he spent his summers with his family. It is in this small hut, a sort of hermitage in the woods that Mahler began to sketch the Ninth Symphony, in the summer of 1908.

In the same period, Mahler also proceeded with his other great work, go and tell The Song of the earth.

The four parts of symphony number 9 are:

1st Andante, Mit Wut (angrily), resolute Allegro, *leidenschaftlich,* Andante tempo
2nd Im Tempo eines gemachlichen Ländlers, Etwas täppisch und sehr derb (In quiet time, *Landler,* Clumsy and very rude)
3rd Rondo - Burleska, Allegro assai, *Sehr Trotzig* (very stubborn) - Adagio
4th Adagio. Sehr langsam und noch zurückhalten (Very slow and still withheld).

Liede das von der Erde (The Song of the Earth)

The *Das Lied von der Erde* is a composition for solo voices and orchestra, composed in 1908 and 1909 in Dobbiaco. The premiere dates back to 20 November 1911 in Monaco of Bavaria directed by Bruno Walter shortly after the composer's death who had disappeared in May. While not a symphony in the classical sense but more a collection of lieder, song of the earth belongs to the official catalogue of the Mahler symphonies, without boasting a number to follow.

The composition is divided into six movements, each one sets to music a Lied belonging to the collection *Die chinesische Flte* by Hans Bethge, published in the fall of 1907. The third text was used by Mahler after Wunderhorn and collections of the poems by Ruckert. Mahler had already introduced the voices in earlier symphonies (the Second, Third, Fourth and Eighth), while in *Das Lied von der Erde* happens for the first time a total integration between the lied and symphony.

As with the eighth lied they are accompanied by the full orchestra.

Symphony for alto, tenor and orchestra
Text taken from: Hans Bethge by *Il flute magico* in Chinese text

1st Das Trinklied vom Jammer der Erde (The toast of the evils of the earth) Cheerful heavy. *(Ganze Takte, nicht schnell)*

2nd Der Einsame im Herbst (Lonely autumn) *Etwas schleichend. Erm͵det*

3rd Von der Jugend (Of Youth) *Behaglich heiter*

4th Von der Schnheit (On Beauty) *Comodo Dolcissimo*

5th Der Trunkene im Fr͵hling (The drunk in the spring) Allegro. *(Keck, aber nicht zu schnell)*

6th Der Abschied (Farewell) *Schwer*

Mahler studied carefully the collection of these Chinese poems, all of ancient ages between 699 and 799 A.D. And in the end he chose seven examples, here is a quick rundown:

▶ The plaque in memory placed on the house occupied by Mahler family in the village of Dobbiaco Alt-Schluderbach.

It recalls that the symphony nr. 9, the number ten and the cycle of Liede Das von der Erde here were composed here in the years 1908-1910.

a) *Das Trinklied vom Jammer der Erde* (The toast of the earth pain, Li Tiai Po) this was the original title for the opera, but it was then replaced with the shorter one which it is known today. Mahler, who intervened Bethge's texts with a few alterations. The sense of poetry deals with themes such as: To be born and live is bad, and all the more heartbreaking is the vision of youth and vital health. Life is dark, death is dark.

b) *Die Einsame im Herbst* (The Lonely autumn, Chang Chi) this second lied offers an opposing view to the above, since its start there is evidence of the change to optimism, nature appears happy and friendly towards man. But this is only because now deception is eternally consumed towards man: the sweetest season is one where nature is about to say goodbye. In this second part we also find the relationships with the famous *Vier letzte Lieder* (Four Last Lieder) by Richard Strauss.

c) *Von der Jugend* (youth) taken from *Der Pavillon aus Porzellan* (The porcelain pavilion, Li Tiai Po) is the scene, reflected in a pond, of three friends who drink and chat, reminiscent of the contemporary work of Puccini's Turandot. The world is soft and precious with colors, gathered in the pavilion of green and white porcelain, it pours another hidden world in the water pool. The work is elegant and refined in which aesthetics plays an important role.

d) *Von der Schonheit* (of beauty) *Am Ufer* (On the shore, Li Tiai Po) is the fleeting crossing point between the strong femininity and mobile virility: the charm of the supreme modesty in which lives an immense sensuality already resigned to give up.

e) *Der Trinker im Frühling* (The drunk in the spring, Li Tiai Po) questions: if life is just a dream, is not drinking and sleeping supreme happiness? It is not important if it's spring outside, and a bird is singing.

f) *Der Abschied* (The Farewell) is the final song which alone takes half the time of the whole symphony. It brings together two poems by Bethge, one from Mong Hao - Jan and the other by Wang Wei. Returning to the sites, it says that the man who is going to go away forever. But where too? The poetry of Mong Hao -Jan describes the waiting of a friend, whilst that of Wang Wei describes the moment of parting. Leave of what (far from where he plays the famous Yiddish fable)? And where do you go? Mahler had some second thoughts about himself, he revised a stateless person who always loved to say: *Bohemian in Austria, between the German and Austrian Jew in the world.* He knows that his alien status in the world is irredeemable.

Von der schönheit (Beauty)

Young girls picking flowers,
Picking lotus flowers at the riverbank.
Amid bushes and leaves they sit,
gathering flowers in their laps and calling
one another in raillery.
Golden sun plays about their form
reflecting them in the clear water.
The sun reflects back their slender limbs,
their sweet eyes,
and the breeze teasing up the warp
of their sleeves, directs the magic
of perfume through the air.

O see, what a tumult of handsome boys
there on the shore on their spirited horses.
Yonder shining like the sun's rays
between the branches of green willows
trot along the bold companions.
The horse of one neighs happily on
and shies and rushes there,
hooves shaking down blooms, grass,
trampling wildly the fallen flowers.
Hei! How frenzied his mane flutters,
and hotly steam his nostrils!
Golden sun plays about their form
reflecting them in the clear water.
And the most beautiful of the maidens sends
long looks adoring at him.
Her proud pose is but a pretense;
in the flash of her big eyes,
in the darkness of her ardent gaze
beats longingly her burning heart.

▲ Mahler and Alma on the deck of the ship that brings them back to Europe for their last trip. The musician was already very ill, and died a few weeks later.

Symphony no. 10 in F sharp major (the crisis symphony)

Symphony no. 10 is the last composition by Gustav Mahler. But it could not be completed. Mahler who foresaw the end, worked intensively on this symphony in the summer of 1910 in Dobbiaco. That was a very dramatic period in the life of the musician.

Just that summer the drama tied to the betrayal of his wife with Walter Gropius exploded, which seriously undermined the spirit of Mahler, enough to lead to his death a year later. This fatal atmosphere is present in this last symphony. In the last summer he was able to complete only the first movement and to work out a remarkable set of notes relating to the construction of the rest of the symphony. With the end of summer he went back to the US for his tenure as conductor. He was unable to complete this work as death overtook him on 18 May 1911.

According to the sketches found after the death of Mahler, the symphony had to be in five movements:

1st Adagio. andante
2nd Scherzo. Schnelle vierteln
3rd Purgatorio oder Inferno. Allegretto moderate
4th Scherzo. Nicht zu schnell Cheerful heavy. *Ider Teufel tanzt es mit Miri* (the dancing devil with me).
5th Final. Einleitung. Langsam, schwer

As I mentioned, after the composer's death only the first movement was completed. The other four movements are less complete as orchestrated only in part (the second and third movement) or in the form of sketches (the last two).

The history of the composition of the Tenth has a curious superstitious component. It is linked to the famous Ninth Symphony, or the unsurpassable limit of nine symphonies produced by any great symphonist of the past. Ninth represented the limit reached e.g. Beethoven, Schubert, and Dvorak Anton Bruckner. Previously the composer had tried to overcome this fact and composed an opera - symphonic Lieder, *Das Lied von der Erde*, which could be referred to as a symphony, but he did not number this one in order not to get too close to the ninth limit too quickly.

After the composer's death the material passed into the hands of Alma who until 1924 did not show this folder to anybody. In that year she subjected the material to an Austrian composer Ernst Krenek, husband of her daughter Anna.

Krenek completed the instrumentation of the third movement based on the sketch of Mahler and the indications given by the sketches. However, in the years following Alma closed like a clam about re-opening this symphony in relation to the enigma of her husband and believed it did not do him justice.

The case was reopened only many years later, in 1949 when Alma gave Arnold Schoenberg the possibility of completing the work, but Schoenberg, tired and sick did not feel up to accepting the assignment. Other musicians tried in the fifties to revive this work and among them should be noted the attempt by the British musician Deryck Cooke. In 1960 he got Alma's permission to carefully examine the original manuscript and readied what he called an executable version of Mahler's sketches related to the tenth. Cooke faced the task with an ethical sense, trying to affix the bare minimum to Mahler sketches, without ever claiming to reconstruct what could have been the author's final will. The first approach developed by Cooke found a firm opposition from Alma, but later she changed her mind acknowledging that the English musicologist had managed to capture the spirit of Mahler.

Over the years, Cooke will produce four different versions of this work. The version of Cooke is now recognized as the most philological and executed, however, it is not the only one. Other tithes are those developed by the American musicologists Clinton Carpenter and Joseph Wheeler. In 1989 another Italian-

American musician Remo Mazzetti introduced its reconstruction.

Finally, in 2001, they were presented almost simultaneously the last two reconstructions of the symphony, by the Russian conductor Rudolf Barshai and the Italian musicologists Nicola Samale and Giuseppe Mazzucca.

Letter of Gustav Mahler to his wife Alma of August 27, 1910

From my bedside in the morning, Toblach
My dear, my lyre,
Come and exorcises the spirits of darkness, they have taken hold of me
Today, they throw me to the ground. Do not leave me, my love
Come early so I can get back.
I lay down and I wait and I ask me
in the silence of my heart if I can still
be saved or whether I am damned.

Herr Mahler hat das Heft jetzt in der Hand
Er wird drum als Beethoven anerkannt.

▲ Caricature of Mahler about tenth symphony. The text says *Mahler has in his hands the project folder that could not even Beethoven ...*

▲ Mahler in the company of the writer Thomas Mann and K. Pringsheim on the streets of Monaco in 1910.

COMPLETE LIST OF MAHLER WORKS

1866   **Polka for piano with a funeral march of introduction** (lost)

1866   **Die Türken** (The Turkish) Lied on: Gotthold Ephraim Lessing (lost)

1875   **Lieder nach Gedichten von Heinrich Heine** (song on text by Heinrich Heine) (lost)

1876   **Sonate für Violine und Klavier** (Sonata for violin and piano) (destroyed by Mahler)

1876   **Nocturne für Cello und Klavier?** (Nocturne for cello and piano) (destroyed by Mahler)

1878   **Klavierquartett a-moll** (Piano Quartet in A minor)

1877-79   **Herzog Ernst von Schwaben** (Duca Ernst von Schwaben) Lirique opera (destroyed by Mahler)

1878   **Klavierquintett** (Piano Quinte in A minor) (lost)

1880   **Das Klagende Lied** (The song of lament and prosecution) Performed in three parts Text: Gustav Mahler

   Waldmärchen (The legend of the forest) - Langsam und träumerisch

   Der Spielmann (The Minstrel) - Mit sehr geheimnisvollem Ausdruck

   Hoch zeitsstuck (The Marriage) - Mit höllischer Wildheit

1879- 1883   **Rübezahl** Opera in five acts Libretto: Gustav Mahler (lost)

1880   **Die Argonauten** (The Argonauts) Opera Libretto: Mahler and Josef Steiner (destroyed by Mahler)

1880   **Drei Lieder** (Three lieder) for tenor and piano on texts by Gustav Mahler. Dedication to J. Poisl

   Im Lenz (in the spring) - F major

   Winterlied (Winter Song) - the largest

   Maitanz im Grünen (Hans and Grete) - D major

1883   **Fünf Lieder und Gesänge aus der Jugendzeit** (Five songs and chants from the youth) (Lieder und Gesänge, vol. I) for voice and piano

   Frühlingsmorgen (Spring Morning) - (F major)

   Erinnerung (Remembrance) - (G minor)

   Hans und Grethe (Hans and Grete) - (D major)

   Serenade aus "Don Juan" (Serenade from Don Juan) - (D flat major)

   Phantasie aus "Don Juan" (Don Juan Fantasy) - (F sharp major)

1882-1883   **Nordische Symphonie** (Nordic Symphony) (lost)

1882-1883   **Symphonie a-moll** (Symphony in A Minor) (lost)

1883   **Vorspiel mit Chor** (Prelude with chorus) (Lost in the bombing of Kassel in 1944)

1884   **Lieder eines fahrenden Gesellen** (Songs of a young traveling) Text: Gustav Mahler

   Wenn mein Schatz Hochzeit macht (When my love will make her marriage) - Schneller. sanft bewegt

   Ging heut 'morgen übers Feld (I went this morning to the campaign) - In gemächlicher Bewegung

   Ich hab 'ein Messer glühend (I have a red-hot knife) - stürmisch, wild

   Die zwei blauen Augen (The blue eyes of my darling) -

1884   **Der Trompeter von Säkkingen** (Tableaux vivants poems for orchestra by Joseph Victor von Scheffel) (Lost under the bombardment of Kassel in 1944).

1888   **Symphony no. 1 in D major "Titan"**

Aus den Tagen der Jugend - Blumen, Frucht und Dornstücke (From the days of youth - Flowers, fruit and spines)

1 Frühling und kein Ende (Spring endlessly) - Einleitung und Allegro comfortable, Die Enleitung Erwachen stellt das aus der Natur langem Winterschlafe give

2 Blumine - Andante Allegretto in C major

3 Mit vollen Segeln (A full sail) - Joke Comedy Humana

4 Gestrandet! Ein Todtenmarsch in "Callots Manier" (Stranded! A funeral march in the manner of Callot)

5 From Hell to Paradise - Allegro furious folgt, als eines der Ausbruch plötzliche im tiefsten verwundeten Herzens

1888   **Todtenfeier** (Rite funeral) symphonic poem for large orchestra by Mahler Designed as a standalone composition, will go to the first half of the Symphony no. 2 in C minor

1888- 1891   **Gesänge aus "Des Knaben Wunderhorn"** (Lieder from "Des Knaben Wunderhorn") (Lieder und Gesange, vol. II) for voice and piano Texts: Ludwig Achim von Arnim and Clemens Brentano

- Um Schlimme artig Kinder zu machen (To turn the bad into good children) - E major
- Ich ging mit Luszt durch einen Wald grunen (allegro I would go for a green forest) - D major
- Aus! Aus! - D flat major
- Starke Einbildungskraft (unbridled Imagination) - is greater memolle
- Zu Strassburg auf der Schanz (at Strasbourg in the trench) - F sharp major
- Ablösung im Sommer (Changing of the guard in the summer) - D flat minor
- Scheiden und Meiden (Divide and set off) - F major
- Nicht Wiedersehen! (Do not see each other ever again) - C minor
- Selbstgefühl (How I feel) - F major

1888-1901   **Gesänge aus "Des Knaben Wunderhorn"** (Lieder from "Des Knaben Wunderhorn") for voice and orchestra or piano ad libitum Text: Ludwig Achim von Arnim and Clemens Brentano "Humoresken" 1892

- Der Schildwache Nachtlied (Night Song of the watchman) - B flat major
- Verlor'ne Müh '! (Wasted effort) - the largest
- Trost im Unglück (Conforto misery) - the largest
- Wer hat dies Liedlein erdacht ?! (Who invented this little song?) - F major
- Himmlische das Leben (The Heavenly Life) - G major

Lieder, Humoresken und ballads, 1892-1901

- Irdische das Leben (Mortality) - G major
- Des Antonius von Padua Fischpredigt (St. Anthony of Padua Preaching to the fish) - C minor
- Urlicht (primigenea Light) - D flat major
- Rheinlegendchen (Little Rhine Legend) - most
- Sungen es drei Engel (Bimm bamm, BIMM, bamm) - F major
- Lob des hohen Verstandes (Praise the high intellect) - D major
- Lied des Verfolgten im Turm (Song of the prisoner in the tower) - D minor
- Wo die schönen Trompeten blasen (Where they play the beautiful trumpets) - D minor
- Revelge (Alarm) - D minor
- Der Tamboursg'sell (The Drummer) - D minor

1899   **Symphonie Nr. 1 in D-Dur "Titan"** (Symphony no. 1 in D major "Titan") final version
    Langsam, schleppend, Wie ein Naturlaut; im Aanfag sehr gemächlich; belebtes Zeitmass
    (Slowly, dragged, like a sound of nature, very quiet at the beginning)
    Kräftig, bewegt, doch nicht zu schnell; Trio, Recht gemächlich
    (Vigorously moved, but not too soon; Trio, very quiet)
    Feierlich und gemessen, ohne zu schleppen
    (Solemn and measured without dragging)
    Stürmisch bewegt. energisch
    (Stormily agitated)

1888-1894 **Symphonie Nr. 2 in c-Moll "Auferstehung"** (Symphony no. 2 in C minor, "Resurrection") five times for soprano and alto soloists, mixed choir and orchestra
    Allegro maestoso. Durchaus ernstem und mit Ausdruck feierlichem
    (Allegro maestoso. With absolutely serious and solemn expression)
    Andante moderato. sehr gemächlich
    (Andante moderate. Very Comfortable)
    In ruhig fließender Bewegung
    (With quiet and smooth movement)
    "Urlicht" (Primeval Light) - Sehr feierlich, aber schlicht, Choralmässig
    (Very solemn but simply, as a choral)
    Im Tempo des Scherzo. Wild herausfahrend. Cheerful energetic. Langsam. Mysterious
    (Joke of Time. Wildly. Energetic Allegro. Slow. Mysterious)
    It contains the hymn "Die Auferstehung" (The Resurrection) by Friedrich Klopstock reworked by Malher

1892-1893 **Lieder eines fahrenden Gesellen** (Songs of a young traveling) Text: Gustav Mahler version for voice and orchestra
    Wenn mein Schatz Hochzeit macht (When my treasure go to a wedding) - Schneller. sanft bewegt
    Ging heut 'morgen übers Feld (I went this morning to the campaign) - In gemächlicher Bewegung
    Ich hab 'ein Messer glühend (I have a red-hot knife) - stürmisch, wild
    Die zwei blauen Augen (The blue eyes of my darling) - Mit geheimnisvoll schwermüthigem Ausdruck. ohne Sentimentalität

1895-1896   **Symphonie Nr. 3 in d-Moll** (Symphony no. 3 in D minor) in six times for alto solo, female choir, children's choir and orchestra
Part I:
    Kräftig.Entschieden (Forcefully, Determined)
Part II:
    minuet time: sehr mässig (minuet time: very moderate)
    Comfortable, jokingly, Ohne Hast (Comodo, Kidding, No hurry)
    Sehr langsam, Mysterious "O Mennsch! gib acht "(Very slow, eerie" Man is 'attentive')
    alto solo from "Also sprach Zarathustra" by Friedrich Nietzsche
    Lustig und im Time keck im Ausdruck "Es sungen drei Engel" (Merrily into the rhythm and lively expression "sang three Angels")
    for alto, female chorus and white divoci chorus from "Des Knaben Wunderhorn"
    Langsam, Ruhevoll, Empfunden (Slow, Quiet, Heard)

1999-1900 **Symphonie Nr. 4 in G-Dur** (Symphony no. 4 in G major) in four times for orchestra and soprano solo

    Bedächtig, Nicht Eilen, recht gemächlich (Thoughtful, not rushed, very convenient)

    Im gemächlicher Bewegung, Ohne Hast (With quiet movement, Unhurried)

    Ruhevoll (Calm)

    Sehr behaglich "himmlische Das Leben" (Very conveniently "The Heavenly Life") for soprano voice from " Des Knaben Wunderhorn"

1901-1902   **Rückert-Lieder** (Five Songs for voice and orchestra) Text: Friedrich Rückert

    Blicke mir nicht in die Lieder (not spy on my songs) - Sehr lebhaft (F major)

    Ich ATMET 'einen linden Duft (I breathed a gentle fragrance) - Sehr zart und innig (D major)

    Ich bin der Welt abhanden gekommen (Lost now I am in the world) - Äußerst langsam und zurückhaltend (F major)

    Um mitternacht (at midnight) - Ruhig, gleichmäßig

    Liebst du um Schoenheit? (Do you love me for the beauty?) - Innig

1901-1903   **Symphonie Nr. 5 in cis-Moll** (Symphony no. 5 in C sharp minor) in five days for orchestra

Part I:

    Trauermarsch. In gemessenem Schritt. Streng. Wie ein Konduit

    (Funeral March, with measured pace, Strictly, as a funeral procession)

    Stürmisch bewegt. Mit größter Vehemenz

    (Stormily moved, with the utmost vehemence)

Part II:

    Joke. Kräftig, nicht zu schnell

    (Scherzo, Vigorous, not too early)

Part III:

    Adagietto. sehr langsam

    (Adagietto, Very slow)

    Rondo-Finale. Cheerful. Cheerful playful. Frisch

    (Rondo-Finale, Allegro, Allegro giocoso, Brioso)

1901-1904   **Kindertotenlieder** (Songs for the dead children) for voice and orchestra Text: Friedrich Rückert

    Nun will die Sonn 'so hell aufgeh'n (And today the sun still wants to rise so bright)

    Langsam und schwermütig; nicht schleppend (D minor)

    Nun seh 'ich wohl, warum so dunkle Flammen (Now I see well why such dark flames)

    Ruhig, nicht schleppend (C minor)

    Wenn dein Mutterlein (When your mommy)

    Schwer, dumpf (C minor)

    Oft denk 'ich, sie sind nur ausgegangen (often think they are just out for a walk)

    Ruhig bewegt, ohne zu Eilen (E flat minor)

    In diesem Wetter (In this weather, in this storm)

    Ruhelos schmerzvollem mit Ausdruck (D minor)

1903-1904 **Symphonie Nr. 6 in a-Moll "Die Tragische"** (Symphony no. 6 in A minor "Tragic")
four times for orchestra
- Cheerful energetic, but not too much
- Joke. Wuchtig
- Andante moderato
- Final. Allegro moderato - Allegro energetic

1904-1905 **Symphonie Nr. 7 in e-Moll**
(Symphony no. 7 in E minor) in five days for orchestra
- Langsam (Adagio). Nicht schleppen - resolute Allegro, ma non troppo
- Nachtmusik. Allegro moderato
- Joke. Schattenhaft - Trio
- Nachtmusik. Andante amoroso
- Rondo-Finale. The time (ordinary Allegro) - Time II (Allegro moderato but energetic)

1906 **Symphonie Nr. 8 in Es-Dur "Symphonie der Tausend"**
(Symphony no. 8 in E flat major "Symphony of a Thousand")
in two times for three sopranos, two altos, tenor, baritone and bass soloists, children's choir, mixed choir and double orchestra
Text: Rabanus Maurus, hymn "Veni Creator"; Johann Wolfgang von Goethe, "Faust" final scene of the tragedy
Part I:
- Hymn "Veni Creator Spiritu" - impetuous Allegro

Part II:
- final scene of Faust by Johann Wolfgang von Goethe - Poco adagio - More moved. (Allegro moderato)

1908 **Das Lied von der Erde** (The Song of the Earth) Symphony in six times for tenor, alto and orchestra
Text: Hans Bethge from "The Magic Flute" of Chinese texts
- Trinklied das vom Jammer der Erde (The evils of the earth toasts) - Allegro heavy. (Ganze Takte, nicht schnell)
- Einsame der im Herbst (Lonely autumn) - Etwas schleichend. ermüdet
- Von der Jugend (Of Youth) - Behaglich heiter
- Von der Schönheit (On Beauty) - Comodo Dolcissimo
- Trunkene der im Frühling (The drunkard in Spring) - Allegro. (Keck, aber nicht zu schnell)
- Der Abschied (Farewell) - Schwer

1909 **Sinfonia Nr. 9 in D-Dur**
(Symphony no. 9 in D major)
four times for orchestra
- Andante, Mit Wut, resolute Allegro, leidenschaftlich, Time The Andante
- Im Tempo eines gemachlichen Ländlers, Etwas täppisch und sehr derb
(In time of a quiet Ländler, a little 'clumsy and very rude)
- Rondo - Burleska, Allegro assai, Sehr Trotzig - Adagio
(Rondo - Burleska, Allegro assai, Very stubborn - Adagio)
- Adagio

1910 **Symphonie Nr. 10 in fis-Moll (Symphony no. 10 in F sharp major)**
five times for orchestra (unfinished)
- Slowly. andante
- Joke. Schnelle vierteln
- Purgatorio oder Inferno. Allegretto moderate
- (Scherzo. Allegro heavy. Nicht zu schnell)
- "Der Teufel tanzt es mit mir"
- Final. Einleitung. (Langsam, schwer)

www.ingramcontent.com/pod-product-compliance
Lightning Source LLC
LaVergne TN
LVHW070446070526
838199LV00037B/699